SUMMER MATH WORKBOOK

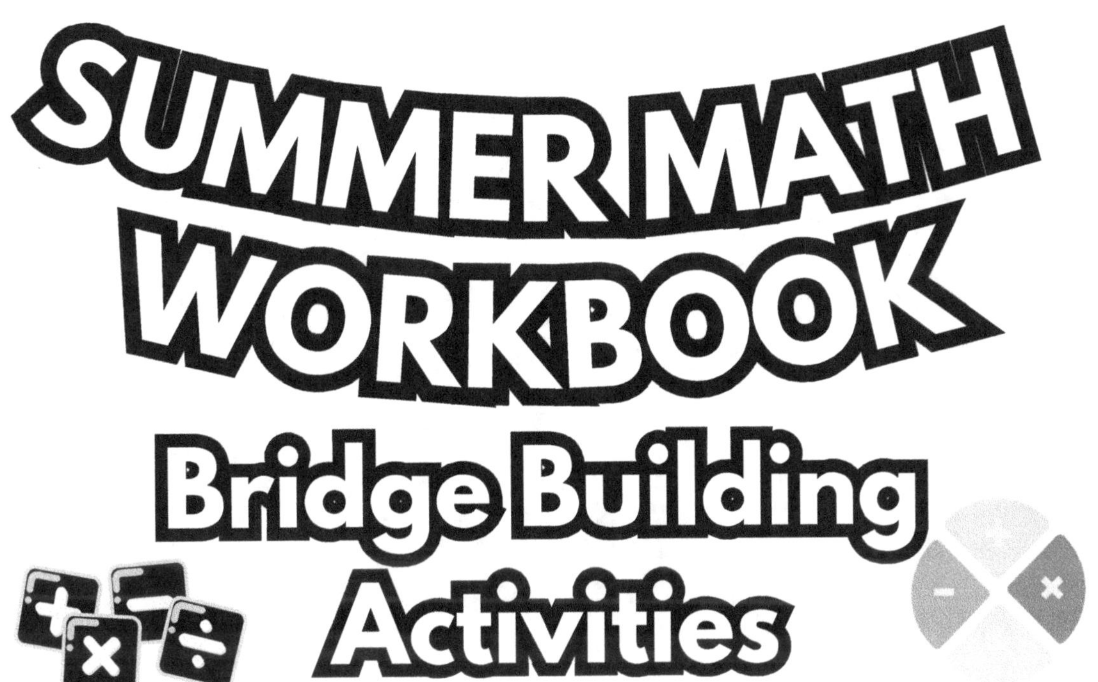

Introduction

As parents and educators, we understand the pivotal role that mathematics plays in shaping a child's academic journey and future success. Yet, the path to mathematical proficiency can often seem daunting, filled with challenges and complexities. That's where the transformative power of Summer Bridge Building Activities books comes into play, illuminating the way forward with clarity, precision, and purpose.

Summer vacation is a time for rest and relaxation, but it also presents the risk of the "summer slide," where students lose some of the academic gains they made during the school year. Summer Bridge Building Activities books are specifically designed to tackle this challenge, ensuring that your child stays academically engaged and prepared for the upcoming school year. These books provide a seamless bridge from one grade to the next, reinforcing essential skills and introducing new concepts that will give your child a head start.

Imagine your child eagerly diving into the pages of a Summer Bridge Building Activities book, greeted by clear, engaging content that demystifies complex mathematical concepts. With each turn of the pages, they embark on a journey of discovery, encountering thoughtfully curated practice questions that reinforce learning and sharpen problem-solving skills. As they unveil the answers to those questions, a sense of accomplishment blossoms within them — a tangible reward for their hard work and dedication.

Summer Bridge Building Activities books transcend traditional educational tools; they are meticulously crafted to build a deep and enduring understanding of mathematics. These books follow a sequential and logical progression, starting from fundamental principles and advancing to sophisticated problem-solving strategies. Each chapter is designed to build on the previous one, ensuring a solid and comprehensive foundation for future learning.

Parents, we yearn for nothing more than to see our children thrive academically and personally. We want to witness the spark of inspiration ignited within them as they overcome academic challenges with confidence and poise. Summer Bridge Building Activities books serve as indispensable partners in this noble endeavor, offering not just practice questions but the keys to unlocking a world of academic and personal opportunities.

Visualize the pride on your child's face as they master a challenging math concept, the joy they experience when their efforts yield results, and the confidence they gain with each success. These pages are designed to make learning math a positive, enriching, and deeply rewarding experience that will benefit them throughout their academic journey and beyond.

For educators, Summer Bridge Building Activities books are invaluable allies in the quest to cultivate mathematical proficiency in the classroom. Accompanied by comprehensive guides and readily available answers, instructors can focus on mentoring and nurturing their students, secure in the knowledge that these books provide a robust framework for effective learning.

Within the pages of Summer Bridge Building Activities books lies not just the promise of academic excellence, but the seeds of a brighter future. By integrating these resources into your child's summer routine, you are bestowing upon them the gifts of confidence, curiosity, and a lifelong love of learning.

Invest in your child's future today with Summer Bridge Building Activities books — because every great journey begins with a single step, and this step can change everything. Keep the momentum of learning alive over the summer, and watch your child soar to new academic heights.

Contents

Grade
1 → 2
SUMMER MATH
WORKBOOK
Bridge Building
Activities
Number Sense
Addition and Subtraction
Place Value

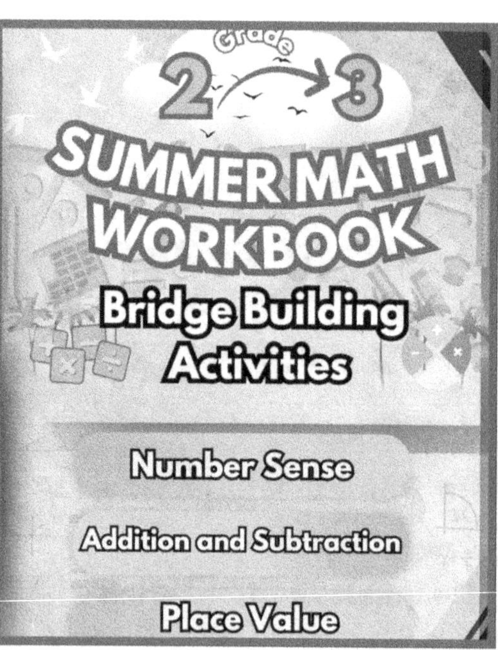

Grade
2 → 3
SUMMER MATH
WORKBOOK
Bridge Building
Activities
Number Sense
Addition and Subtraction
Place Value

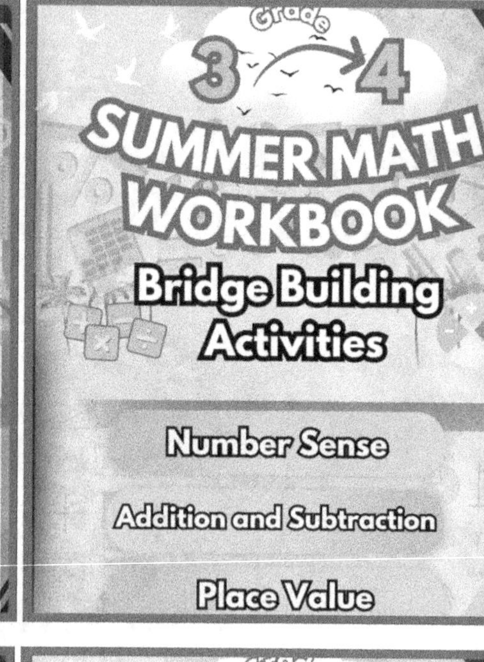

Grade
3 → 4
SUMMER MATH
WORKBOOK
Bridge Building
Activities
Number Sense
Addition and Subtraction
Place Value

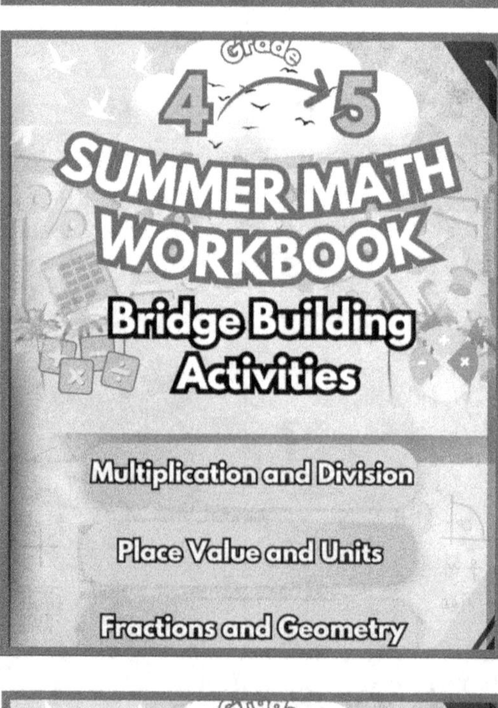

Grade
4 → 5
SUMMER MATH
WORKBOOK
Bridge Building
Activities
Multiplication and Division
Place Value and Units
Fractions and Geometry

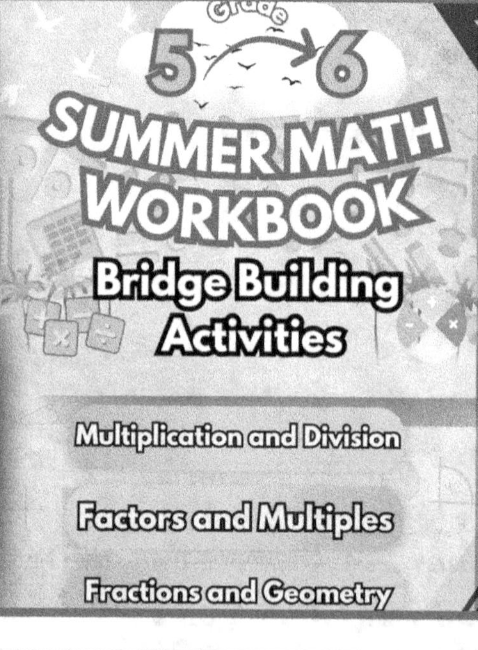

Grade
5 → 6
SUMMER MATH
WORKBOOK
Bridge Building
Activities
Multiplication and Division
Factors and Multiples
Fractions and Geometry

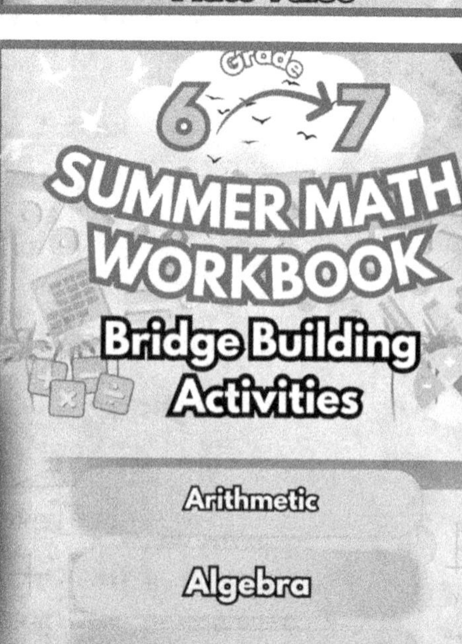

Grade
6 → 7
SUMMER MATH
WORKBOOK
Bridge Building
Activities
Arithmetic
Algebra
Geometry and Statistics

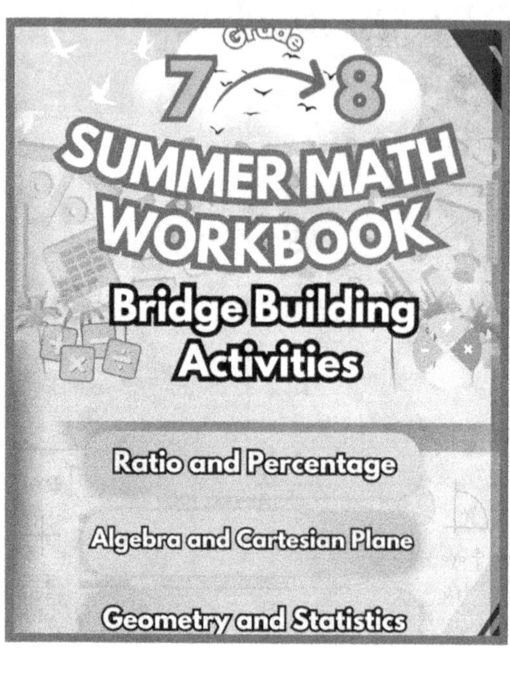

Grade
7 → 8
SUMMER MATH
WORKBOOK
Bridge Building
Activities
Ratio and Percentage
Algebra and Cartesian Plane
Geometry and Statistics

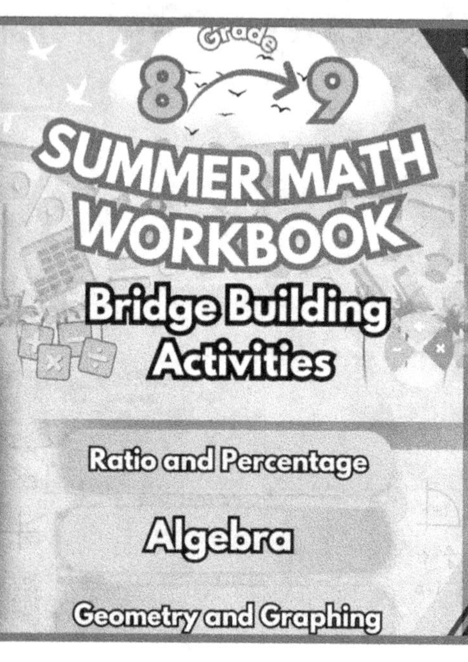

Grade
8 → 9
SUMMER MATH
WORKBOOK
Bridge Building
Activities
Ratio and Percentage
Algebra
Geometry and Graphing

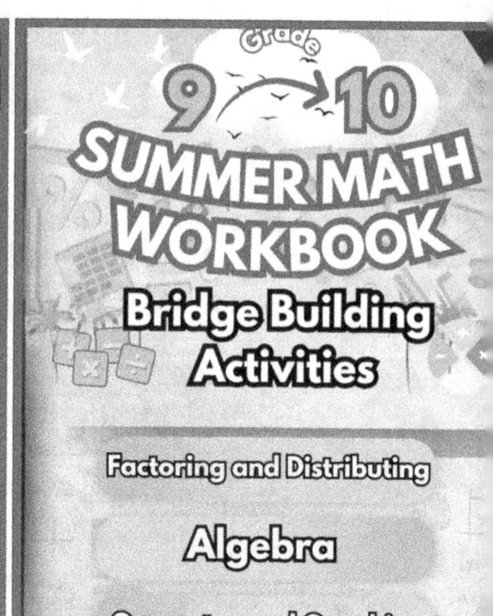

Grade
9 → 10
SUMMER MATH
WORKBOOK
Bridge Building
Activities
Factoring and Distributing
Algebra
Geometry and Graphing

<u>**Multiplication and Division**</u>

Multiplication

Multiplication is an easy way of adding numbers together quickly. Instead of adding the same number repeatedly, we use multiplication to find the total much faster.

For instance, rather than adding 2 + 2 + 2 + 2 + 2, we can multiply 2 by 5 to get the same result: 2 x 5 = 10.

Here, the first number (2) is called the multiplicand, second number (5) is the multiplier. The answer we get, in this case, 10, is called the product.

Let's think of multiplication as repeated addition.

Take 2 x 5, for example. It means adding 2 together five times, which we can illustrate as: 2 + 2 + 2 + 2 + 2 = 10

Multiplication can also be visualized as groups of objects. Imagine we have 2 groups, each containing 5 oranges.

To find the total number of oranges, we multiply the number of groups (2) by the number of oranges in each group (5):

2 groups of 5 oranges = 10 oranges

Expressed as multiplication: 2 x 5 = 10

In summary, multiplication offers various ways to approach it: through repeated addition or by envisioning groups of objects. It's a powerful tool that makes solving math problems much quicker and more efficient!

Long Division and Remainders

Division is like the opposite of multiplication. It's all about sharing or distributing items equally among a certain number of groups or people.

When we divide one number by another, we're essentially splitting a number into equal parts. We're figuring out how many groups of a certain size can be made from that number.

For instance, let's divide 20 by 4.

When we divide 20 by 4, we're essentially asking, "How many groups of size 4 can we make from 20?"

Now, there are several parts or terms involved in the division process:

- **Dividend:** This is the number being divided, which in this case, is 20.

- **Divisor:** This is the number we're dividing by, which is 4.

- **Quotient:** This is the answer we get after dividing. It tells us how many groups of divisors can be made from the dividend. In this case, the answer is 5.

- **Remainder:** when the divisor doesn't evenly divide the dividend, we get the remainder.

So, when we divide 20 by 4, we found out that 5 groups of 4 can be made from 20.

Let's solve problems from exercises:

$$\begin{array}{r} 08{,}464.6 \\ 10\,)\overline{\,84{,}646} \\ -0 \\ \hline 84 \\ -80 \\ \hline 46 \\ -40 \\ \hline 64 \\ -60 \\ \hline 46 \\ -40 \\ \hline 60 \\ -60 \\ \hline 0 \end{array}$$

$$\begin{array}{r} 8{,}965 \text{ R1} \\ 9\,)\overline{\,80{,}686} \\ -72 \\ \hline 86 \\ -81 \\ \hline 58 \\ -54 \\ \hline 46 \\ -45 \\ \hline 1 \end{array}$$

Multi Digit Multiplication

$$\begin{array}{r} 70{,}278 \\ \times \quad 2{,}965 \\ \hline +\quad 351390 \\ +\quad 421668 \\ +\ 632502 \\ +140556 \\ \hline =208374270 \end{array}$$

Multiplying Decimals

Multiplying decimals is a lot like multiplying whole numbers, but we need to be careful about where we put the decimal point in the answer.

Step 1: Start by multiplying the numbers together, just like we do with whole numbers. Ignore the decimals for now.

Step 2: Count how many decimal places there are in the numbers we're multiplying. This will tell us how many decimal places our answer should have.

Step 3: Put the decimal point in the answer by starting from the right side of the number. Move the decimal point to the left as many places as there are in the total number of decimal places.

For example, let's multiply 4.5 by 2.5:

Step 1: Multiply the numbers as if they were whole numbers:

$$25 \times 45 = 1125.$$

Step 2: There is one decimal place in 2.5 and one in 4.5, making a total of two decimal places.

Step 3: Starting from the right side of the answer, count two places to the left and put the decimal point there.

So, the final answer is 11.25.

Remember to pay close attention to where the decimal point goes in the answer.

Dividing Decimals

Dividing decimals is a lot like dividing whole numbers, but we need to be careful about placement of decimal point in the answer.

Steps to follow:

1. **Set up the division problem:** Write the dividend (the number being divided) and the divisor (the number you're dividing by) as you would in a long division problem.

$$1.7 \overline{)1.6}$$

2. **Move the decimal:** Move the decimal point to the right in the dividend and divisor by the same number of places.

$$17 \overline{)16}$$

3. **Perform the division:** Divide as you would with whole numbers.

```
        0 0.9 4
   17)16
      - 0
       16
      - 0
       16 0
    -15 3
         7 0
       - 6 8
           2
```

4. **Place the decimal point:** Place the decimal point in the quotient directly above its position in the dividend.

So, the quotient is 0.94.

<u>**Place Value and Expanded Notations**</u>

Place value tells us the value of a digit in a number based on where it's placed.

Consider the number **45,368,348.86342**. It consists of thirteen digits: 4, 5, 3, 6, 8, 3, 4, 8, 8, 6, 3, 4, and 2.

Digit	Place Value Position	Value Calculation	Value
4	Ten millions place	4 × 10,000,000	40,000,000
5	Millions place	5 × 1,000,000	5,000,000
3	Hundred thousands place	3 × 100,000	300,000
6	Ten thousands place	6 × 10,000	60,000
8	Thousands place	8 × 1,000	8,000
3	Hundreds place	3 × 100	300
4	Tens place	4 × 10	40
8	Ones place	8 × 1	8
8	Tenths place	8 × 0.1	0.8
6	Hundredths place	6 × 0.01	0.06
3	Thousandths place	3 × 0.001	0.003
4	Ten-thousandths place	4 × 0.0001	0.0004
2	Hundred-thousandths place	2 × 0.00001	0.00002

Each digit occupies a unique position:

- The digit **4** is in the ten millions place, signifying four groups of 10,000,000.

- The digit **5** is in the millions place, indicating five groups of 1,000,000.

- The digit **3** is in the hundred thousands place, representing three groups of 100,000.

- The digit **6** is in the ten thousands place, representing six groups of 10,000.

- The digit **8** is in the thousands place, representing eight groups of 1,000.

- The digit **3** is in the hundreds place, representing three groups of 100.

- The digit **4** is in the tens place, representing four groups of 10.

- The digit **8** is in the ones place, representing eight single units.

- The digit **8** is in the tenths place, representing eight groups of 0.1.

- The digit **6** is in the hundredths place, representing six groups of 0.01.

- The digit **3** is in the thousandths place, representing three groups of 0.001.

- The digit **4** is in the ten-thousandths place, representing four groups of 0.0001.

- The digit **2** is in the hundred-thousandths place, representing two groups of 0.00001.

  To find the total value of the number **45,368,348.86342**, we calculate the value of each digit based on its place:

- The digit **4** in the ten millions place equals 40,000,000.

- The digit **5** in the millions place equals 5,000,000.

- The digit **3** in the hundred thousands place equals 300,000.

- The digit **6** in the ten thousands place equals 60,000.

- The digit **8** in the thousands place equals 8,000.

- The digit **3** in the hundreds place equals 300.

- The digit **4** in the tens place equals 40.

- The digit **8** in the ones place equals 8.

- The digit **8** in the tenths place equals 0.8.

- The digit **6** in the hundredths place equals 0.06.

- The digit **3** in the thousandths place equals 0.003.

- The digit **4** in the ten-thousandths place equals 0.0004.

- The digit **2** in the hundred-thousandths place equals 0.00002.

By summing these values, we determine the overall value of the number:

40,000,000 + 5,000,000 + 300,000 + 60,000 + 8,000 + 300 + 40 + 8 + 0.8 + 0.06 + 0.003 + 0.0004 + 0.00002 = 45,368,348.86342

<h1 style="text-align:center"><u>Factors and Multiples</u></h1>

Factors and multiples are two fundamental concepts in mathematics.

Factors:

- Factors are numbers that divide another number without leaving a remainder.

- For example, the factors of 12 are 1, 2, 3, 4, 6, and 12 because these numbers can divide 12 evenly.

- Factors always come in pairs, except for perfect squares.

Multiples:

- Multiples are the result of multiplying a number by an integer.

- For example, the multiples of 3 are 3, 6, 9, 12, 15, and so on because these numbers are obtained by multiplying 3 by 1, 2, 3, 4, 5, and so on.

- Every number has an infinite number of multiples.

Every factor of a number is a divisor of that number, and every multiple of a number is divisible by that number.

Let's solve some problems:

Factors of **44**

2, 4, 11, 22

Multiples of **77**

77, 154, 231, 308, 385

Fractions

Fractions represent parts of a whole. They consist of a numerator (the number on top) and a denominator (the number on the bottom).

For example: we have an orange, and we divide it into 5 equal slices. Each slice represents $\frac{1}{5}$ of the orange. Now, if we take 3 of those slices, we have taken $\frac{3}{5}$ of the orange.

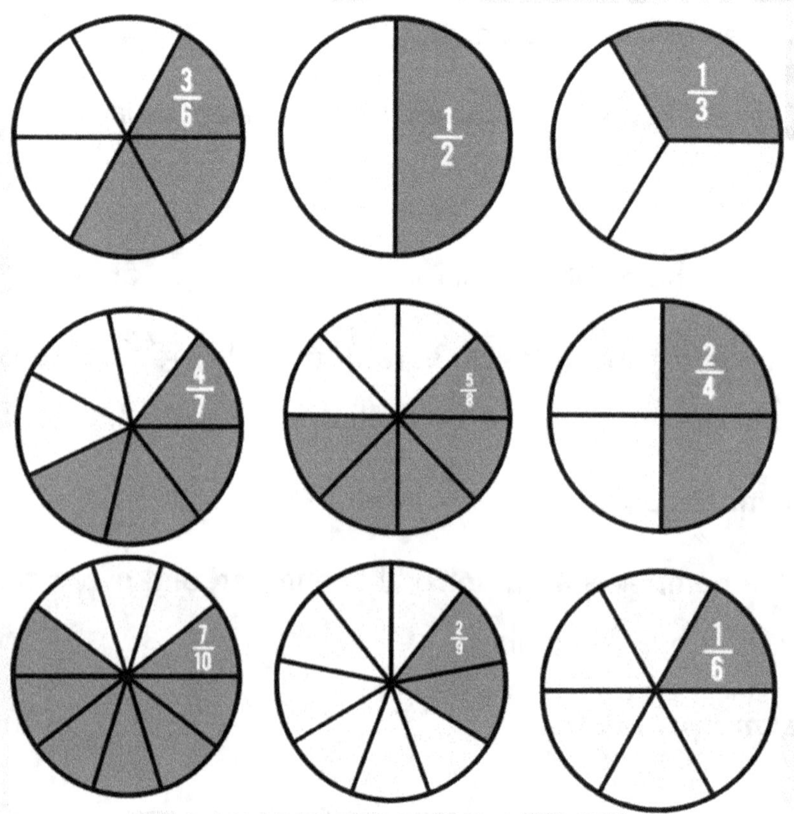

Equivalent Fractions

Equivalent fractions are fractions that represent the same value or part of a whole, even though they may look different.

To find equivalent fractions, you can:

- Multiply or divide both the numerator and denominator by the same nonzero number.
- Simplify fractions to their simplest form.

$\frac{1}{2}$ and $\frac{2}{4}$ are equivalent fractions because if you multiply the numerator and denominator of $\frac{1}{2}$ by 2, you get $\frac{2}{4}$. Similarly, if you divide both the numerator and denominator of $\frac{2}{4}$ by 2, you get $\frac{1}{2}$.

Let's solve a problem:

$$\frac{}{8} = \frac{15}{40}$$

To solve the missing numerator, we can cross multiply.

$$40x = 8 \times 15$$

$$40x = 120$$

$$x = \frac{120}{40} = x = 3$$

$$\frac{3}{8} = \frac{15}{40}$$

<u>**Convert Fractions and Decimals**</u>

Fraction to Decimal

To transform a fraction into a decimal, we divide the numerator by the denominator.

For instance, $\frac{1}{4}$ equals 0.25 because when we divide 1 by 4, we get 0.25.

In certain cases, the resulting decimal repeats infinitely, like $\frac{1}{3}$, which equals 0.3333... In such instances, we round the decimal to a specific number of decimal places.

$$\frac{498}{500} = \frac{498 \div 2}{500 \div 2} = \frac{249}{250} = 0.996$$

Decimal to Fraction

Step 1: Write down the decimal as a fraction with the decimal part in the numerator and the place value of the last digit in the denominator.

Step 2: Simplify the fraction if possible.

For example,

$$0.68 = \frac{17}{25}$$

$$\frac{0.68}{1} = \frac{0.68 \times 100}{1 \times 100} = \frac{68}{100} = \frac{68 \div 4}{100 \div 4}$$

Least Common Multiple (LCM)

The Lowest Common Multiple (LCM) of two or more numbers is the smallest multiple that is divisible by each of the numbers.

There are several methods to find the LCM; however, we will focus on only two:

Listing Multiples: List the multiples of each number until you find a common multiple. For example:

$$\begin{array}{l} 8 \quad 8, 16, 24, 32, 40, 48, 56 \\ \hline 7 \quad 7, 14, 21, 28, 35, 42, 49, 56 \end{array} \quad , \ LCM = \underline{56}$$

Division Method: Divide each number with the smallest prime number that divides at least one of the numbers evenly. The product of all the divisors and quotients is the LCM. For example:

$$
\begin{array}{c|cc}
2 & 7 & 8 \\
\hline
2 & 7 & 4 \\
\hline
2 & 7 & 2 \\
\hline
7 & 7 & 1 \\
\hline
  & 1 & 1
\end{array}
$$

LCM = 2 x 2 x 2 x 7 = <u>56</u>

Both methods have their advantages. For big numbers, using the division way is usually faster. But if we are working with smaller numbers or like seeing patterns, listing multiples might make more sense.

<u>Mixed Numbers: Mixed into Improper</u>

Mixed numbers and improper fractions are two different ways to represent the same value of a fraction.

1. **Mixed Number:** A mixed number is a combination of a whole number and a proper fraction. For example, $2\frac{1}{3}$ is a mixed number, where 2 is the whole number part and $\frac{1}{3}$ is the fraction part.

2. **Improper Fraction:** An improper fraction is a fraction where the numerator is greater than or equal to the denominator. For example, $\frac{7}{3}$ is an improper fraction because 6 is greater than 3.

To convert a mixed number to an improper fraction, you multiply the whole number by the denominator of the fraction, add the numerator, and then write the result over the original denominator. For example:

$$2\frac{1}{3} = \frac{2 \times 3 + 1}{3} = \frac{7}{3}$$

To convert an improper fraction to a mixed number, we divide the numerator by the denominator. The quotient becomes the whole number part, and the remainder becomes the numerator of the fraction. For example:

$$\frac{7}{3} = 2\frac{1}{3}$$

Let's solve some problems:

$$2\frac{10}{20} = \frac{20 \times 2 = 40}{40 + 10 = 50} = \frac{50}{20} = \frac{5}{2}$$

$$\frac{91}{14} = \frac{91 \div 7 = 13}{14 \div 7 = 2} = 6\frac{1}{2}$$

$$13 \div 2 = 6 \text{ with a remainder of 1}$$

Mixed Numbers: Addition and Subtraction

To add or subtract mixed numbers, we follow similar steps as when adding or subtracting regular fractions. For instance:

Addition:

- <u>Add the whole numbers:</u> Add the whole number parts of the mixed numbers together.
- <u>Add the fractions:</u> Add the fractions parts of the mixed numbers together.
- <u>Simplify (if needed):</u> If the fraction part of the sum is an improper fraction, simplify it by converting it to a mixed number.

Subtraction:

- <u>Subtract the whole numbers:</u> Subtract the whole number part of the second mixed number from the whole number part of the first mixed number.
- <u>Subtract the fractions:</u> Subtract the fraction part of the second mixed number from the fraction part of the first mixed number.
- <u>Simplify (if needed):</u> If the fraction part of the difference is a negative fraction, borrow from the whole number part or simplify it by converting it to a mixed number.

Let's solve some problems:

$$3\frac{4}{8} + 7\frac{1}{3} = \frac{4}{8} + \frac{1}{3} = \frac{4\times3 + 8\times1}{8\times3} = \frac{12 + 8}{24} = \frac{20}{24} = 10\frac{5}{6}$$

$$3 + 7 = 10$$

$$7\frac{4}{6} - 2\frac{3}{8} = \frac{4}{6} - \frac{3}{8} = \frac{4\times8 - 6\times3}{6\times8} = \frac{32 - 18}{48} = \frac{14}{48} = 5\frac{7}{24}$$

$$7 - 2 = 5$$

Mixed Numbers: Multiplication and Division

To multiply or divide mixed numbers, we follow these steps:

Multiplication:

- <u>Convert the mixed numbers to improper fractions:</u> Multiply the whole number by the denominator of the fraction, then add the numerator. Write the result over the original denominator.

- <u>Multiply the fractions:</u> Multiply the numerators together to get the new numerator and multiply the denominators together to get the new denominator.
- <u>Simplify (if needed):</u> If the result is an improper fraction, simplify it by converting it back to a mixed number.

Division:

- <u>Convert the mixed numbers to improper fractions:</u>
- <u>Invert the divisor:</u> Flip the second fraction (the one you're dividing by) so that the division becomes multiplication.
- <u>Multiply the fractions:</u> Multiply the numerators together to get the new numerator and multiply the denominators together to get the new denominator.
- <u>Simplify (if needed):</u> If the result is an improper fraction, simplify it by converting it back to a mixed number.

Let's solve some problems:

$$1\frac{2}{4} \times 3\frac{1}{6} = \frac{3}{2} \times \frac{19}{6} = \frac{3 \times 19}{2 \times 6} = \frac{57}{12} = 4\frac{3}{4}$$

$$1 \times 4 + 2 = 6 = \frac{6}{2} = \frac{3}{2} \qquad 3 \times 8 + 1 = \frac{19}{6}$$

$$2\frac{6}{10} \div 6\frac{6}{7} = \frac{13}{5} \times \frac{7}{48} = \frac{13 \times 7}{5 \times 48} = \frac{91}{240}$$

$$2 \times 10 + 6 = 26 = \frac{26}{10} = \frac{13}{5} \qquad 6 \times 7 + 6 = 48 = \frac{48}{7}$$

Multiplication with whole numbers

To multiply a fraction by a whole number, we simply multiply the numerator of the fraction by the whole number while keeping the denominator the same.

For example, if we have $\frac{2}{3}$ and we want to multiply it by 5:

$$5 \times \frac{2}{3} = \frac{5 \times 2}{3} = \frac{10}{3}$$

Let's solve a problem:

$$1 \times \frac{8}{10} = \frac{1 \times 8}{10} = \frac{8 \div 2}{10 \div 2} = \frac{4}{5}$$

Simplify Fractions

To simplify a fraction means to rewrite it in its simplest form, where the numerator and denominator have no common factors other than 1. We follow these steps:

- **Identify the Greatest Common Divisor (GCD):** Find the largest number that divides both the numerator and the denominator evenly.
- **Divide by the GCD:** Divide both the numerator and denominator by their GCD.

For example, let's simplify. $\frac{12}{18}$

Identify the GCD: The factors of 12 are 1, 2, 3, 4, 6, and 12. The factors of 18 are 1, 2, 3, 6, 9, and 18. The largest number that divides both 12 and 18 evenly is 6. So, the GCD is 6.

Divide by the GCD: Divide both the numerator and denominator by 6.

$$\frac{12}{18} \div \frac{6}{6} = \frac{2}{3}$$

Another way to simplify fractions is to factorize the numerator and denominator completely, and then cancel out common factors. This method is particularly useful when dealing with larger numbers or algebraic fractions.

Geometry

Area and Perimeter

The area of a shape represents the amount of space it occupies. The perimeter of a shape is the total distance around its outer edge.

Area of Rectangle

For a square, since all four sides are equal, we only need to know the length of one side to find its area. We can calculate the area of a square by multiplying the length of one side by itself (squared). So, if the length of one side of the square is 's', then the area (A) is given by:

$$A = s \times s$$

4 in

4 in

$$A = 4 \times 4$$

$$A = 16$$

Perimeter of Rectangle

For a square, since all four sides are equal, we can find the perimeter by adding up the lengths of all four sides. If 's' represents the length of one side, then the perimeter (P) is given by:

$$P = 4 \times s$$

$$P = 4 \times 4$$

$$P = 16$$

Area of Triangle:

The area of a triangle represents the amount of space enclosed within its three sides. The formula for calculating the area of a triangle depends on the type of triangle. For a general triangle, we use the formula:

$$A = \frac{1}{2} \times base \times height$$

Where:

- *A* represents the area of the triangle.

- The base is the length of any one side of the triangle.

- The height is the perpendicular distance from the base to the opposite vertex.

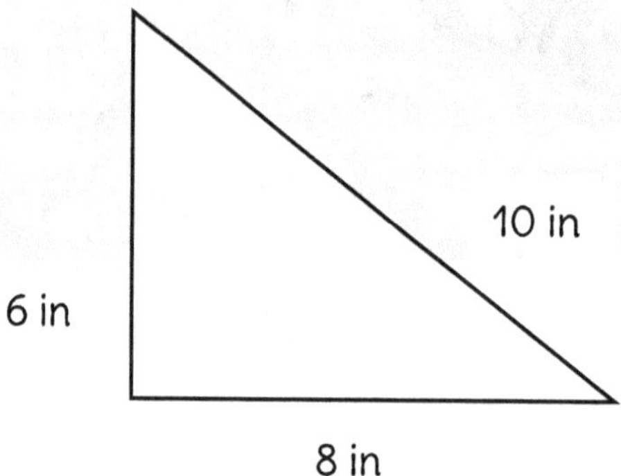

$$A = \frac{1}{2} \times \text{base} \times \text{height}$$

$$A = \frac{1}{2} \times 6 \times 8$$

$$A = \frac{1}{2} \times 48$$

$$A = 24$$

Perimeter of Triangle:

The perimeter of a triangle is the total length of its three sides. To find the perimeter, we simply add the lengths of all three sides together:

$$P = \text{side1} + \text{side2} + \text{side3}$$

$$P = 6 + 8 + 10$$

$$P = 24$$

Equilateral Triangle

An equilateral triangle is a triangle in which all three sides are equal in length. To find the area and perimeter of an equilateral triangle, we can use the following formulas:

- Area (A): $\frac{\sqrt{3}}{4} \times a^2$ where a is the length of one side of the equilateral triangle.
- Perimeter (P): $P = 3a$ where a is the length of one side of the equilateral triangle.

Area of Equilateral Triangle:

$$\text{Area (A): } \frac{\sqrt{3}}{4} \times (6)^2$$

$$\text{Area (A): } \frac{\sqrt{3}}{4} \times 36$$

$$\text{Area (A): } \frac{36\sqrt{3}}{4}$$

$$\text{Area (A): } \frac{36(1.73)}{4}$$

$$\text{Area (A): } \frac{62.35}{4}$$

$$\text{Area (A): } 15.59 \text{ in}^2$$

Perimeter of Equilateral Triangle:

$$P = 3a$$

$$P = 3(6) = 18$$

Isosceles Triangle

An isosceles triangle is a triangle with at least two sides of equal length. The angles opposite the equal sides are also equal.

Area of Isosceles Triangle

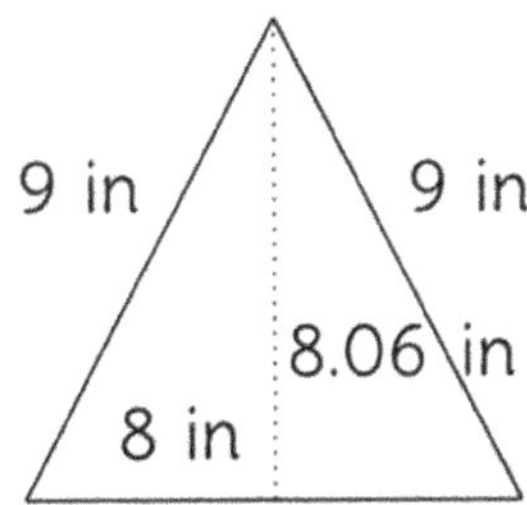

$$A = \frac{1}{2} \times \text{base} \times \text{height}$$

$$A = \frac{1}{2} \times 8 \times 8$$

$$A = \frac{1}{2} \times 64$$

$$A = 32$$

Perimeter of Isosceles Triangle

The perimeter of a triangle is the total length of its three sides. To find the perimeter, we simply add the lengths of all three sides together:

$$P = \text{side1} + \text{side2} + \text{side3}$$

$$P = 9 + 9 + 8$$

$$P = 26$$

Scalene Triangle

A scalene triangle is a triangle with no equal sides and no equal angles. The formula for finding various properties of a scalene triangle is as follows:

Area (A): The area of a scalene triangle can be calculated using Heron's fo rmula, which is given by:

$$A = \sqrt{s(s-a)(s-b)(s-c)}$$

where s is the semi-perimeter of the triangle,

and a, b, and c are the lengths of its three sides.

Perimeter (P): The perimeter of a scalene triangle is the sum of the lengths of its three sides.

$$P = side1 + side2 + side3$$

Let's find the Area and Perimeter of a Scalene Triangle:

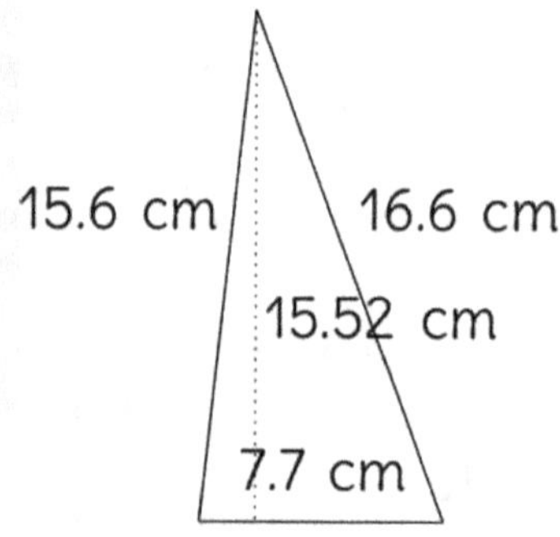

Area (A): First, we calculate the semi-perimeter (s):

$$S = \frac{a+b+c}{2} = \frac{15.6 + 16.6 + 7.7}{2} = \frac{39.8}{2} = 19.9 \text{ cm}$$

Heron's formula to find the area:

$$A = \sqrt{s(s-a)(s-b)(s-c)}$$

$$A = \sqrt{19.9\,(19.9 - 15.6)\,(19.9 - 16.6)\,(19.9 - 7.7)}$$

$$A = \sqrt{19.9 \times 4.3 \times 3.3 \times 12.2}$$

$$A = \sqrt{3445} \approx 59$$

$$P = side1 + side2 + side3$$

$$P = 15.6 + 16.6 + 7.7$$

$$P = 39.8$$

Area and Perimeter of an L-shape

The L-shaped figure typically consists of two rectangles joined together to form an L-shape. To find the area and perimeter of an L-shaped figure, we will need to calculate the areas and perimeters of each rectangle and then combine them.

Area=Area of Rectangle 1 + Area of Rectangle 2

Perimeter=Perimeter of Rectangle 1 + Perimeter of Rectangle 2

Let's find the Area and Perimeter of an L-shape:

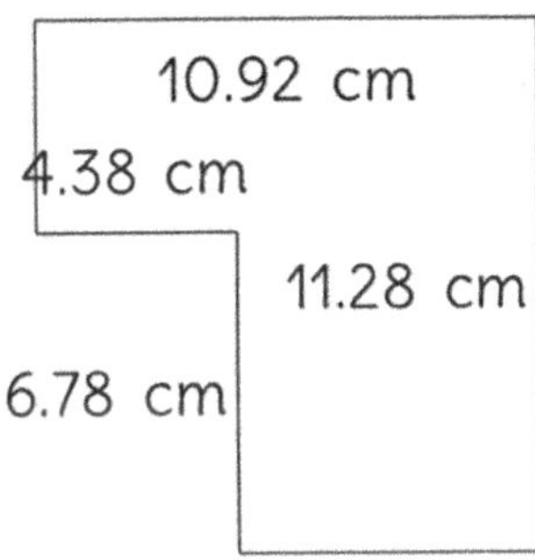

Area of L-Shape

$$\text{Area 1} = 4.38 \times 4.5 = 19.7 \text{ cm}^2$$

$$\text{Area 2} = 11.28 \times 6.54 = 73.7 \text{ cm}^2$$

$$\text{Area} = 19.7 + 73.7$$

$$Area = 93.481 \text{ cm}^2$$

Perimeter of L-Shape

$$P = 11.28 + 6.54 + 6.78 + 4.38 + 4.5 + 10.92$$

$$P = 44.4 \text{ cm}$$

Area and Circumference of circles

To find the area (A) and circumference (C) of a circle, we use the following formulas:

1. **Area of a Circle (A)** $= \pi \times (radius)^2$
   - where π (pi) is a constant with value of (3.14). It is a ratio of the circumference of a circle to its diameter,
   - the radius (r) is the distance from the center of the circle.
2. **Circumference of a Circle (C)** $= 2 \times \pi \times radius$

Let's solve an example: suppose a swimming pool has a radius of 11 meters, we are required to calculate its Area and Circumference:

$$\textbf{Area } (A) = \pi \times (radius)^2$$

$$A = 3.14 \times 11^2$$

$$A = 3.14 \times 121$$

$$A = 379.94 \text{ square meters}$$

$$\textbf{Circumference } (C) = 2 \times \pi \times radius$$

$$C = 2 \times 3.14 \times 11$$

$$C = 69.08 \text{ square meters}$$

<u>**Angles**</u>

Types of Angles: Angles can be classified based on their measures:

- **Acute Angle:** An angle less than 90°.

- **Right Angle:** An angle exactly equal to 90°.

- **Obtuse Angle:** An angle greater than 90° and less than 180°.

- **Straight Angle:** An angle exactly equal to 180°.

- **Reflex Angle:** An angle greater than 180° and less than 360°.

- **Full Angle:** An angle equal to 360°.

Measure angles with a protractor. It looks like a semicircle or a half-disc with degree markings from 0° to 180°.To measure an angle using a protractor, we place the center of the protractor at the vertex of the angle, align one side of the angle with the zero mark on the protractor, and read the degree measure where the other side intersects the protractor.

For example, let's measure the following angle.

The angle is 140°.

We also know that the angle is greater than 90° and less than 180°, so this is an Obtuse angle.

<u>Unit Conversion</u>

Metric Conversion

1 meter (m) = 100 centimeters (cm)

1 meter (m) = 1000 millimeters (mm)

1 kilometer (km) = 1000 meters (m)

1 hectare (ha) = 10000 square meters (m^2)

1 square meter (m^2) = 10000 square centimeters (cm^2)

1 cubic meter (m^3) = 1000 liters (L)

Weights and Measures

1 kilogram (kg) = 1000 grams (g)

1 liter (L) = 1000 milliliters (mL)

1 tonne (t) = 1000 kilograms (kg)

1 centimeter (cm) = 10 millimeters (mm)

1 gram (g) = 1000 milligrams (mg)

1 kilometer (km) = 100000 centimeters (cm)

Statistics

Mean

The mean, also known as the average, is a measure of central tendency.

To find the mean of a set of numbers:

- Add up all the numbers in the set.
- Divide the sum by the total count of numbers in the set.

For example: consider the set of numbers: 70, 72, 49, 69, 27, 76.

$$\text{Mean} = \frac{70 + 72 + 49 + 69 + 27 + 76}{6}$$

$$= \frac{363}{6} = 60.5$$

Median

The median is a measure of central tendency that represents the middle value of a dataset when the values are arranged in ascending or descending order.

To find the median of a set of numbers:

- Arrange the numbers in ascending or descending order.
- If the total count of numbers is odd, the median is the middle value.
- If the total count of numbers is even, the median is the average of the two middle values.

For example: consider the set of numbers: 70, 72, 49, 69, 27, 76.

$$27, 49, 69, 70, 72, 76$$

$$\text{Median} = \frac{69 + 70}{2} = \frac{139}{2} = 69.5$$

Long Division: Remainders

Find the quotient.

1)

$$15\overline{)46{,}998}$$

2)

$$13\overline{)10{,}469}$$

3)

$$16\overline{)78{,}260}$$

4)

$$18\overline{)34{,}790}$$

5)

$$14\overline{)52{,}475}$$

6)

$$12\overline{)78{,}784}$$

7)

$$10\overline{)60{,}593}$$

8)

$$19\overline{)15{,}349}$$

9)

$$3 \overline{)\ 42{,}627}$$

10)

$$19 \overline{)\ 99{,}911}$$

11)

$$3 \overline{)\ 14{,}895}$$

12)

$$13 \overline{)\ 64{,}157}$$

13)

12) 50,524

14)

2) 22,587

15)

3) 91,372

16)

2) 18,436

17)

13)74,854

18)

13)81,429

19)

10)84,217

20)

13)48,693

Multi Digit Multiplication

Find the product.

1)
$$\begin{array}{r} 36{,}892 \\ \times\ 1{,}087 \\ \hline \end{array}$$

2)
$$\begin{array}{r} 99{,}646 \\ \times\ 3{,}449 \\ \hline \end{array}$$

3)
$$\begin{array}{r} 59{,}825 \\ \times\ 7{,}624 \\ \hline \end{array}$$

4)
$$\begin{array}{r} 61{,}838 \\ \times\ 1{,}006 \\ \hline \end{array}$$

5)
$$\begin{array}{r} 23{,}625 \\ \times\ 8{,}585 \\ \hline \end{array}$$

6)
$$\begin{array}{r} 54{,}433 \\ \times\ 2{,}168 \\ \hline \end{array}$$

7)
$$\begin{array}{r} 60{,}086 \\ \times\ 4{,}348 \\ \hline \end{array}$$

8)
$$\begin{array}{r} 50{,}091 \\ \times\ 4{,}117 \\ \hline \end{array}$$

9)
$$\begin{array}{r} 18{,}724 \\ \times\ 4{,}431 \\ \hline \end{array}$$

10) 26,225
   × 2,919
   —————

11) 68,854
   × 3,407
   —————

12) 11,058
   × 4,862
   —————

13) 62,885
   × 7,847
   —————

14) 85,668
   × 9,775
   —————

15) 67,325
   × 5,138
   —————

16) 18,639
   × 9,332
   —————

17) 66,206
   × 4,326
   —————

18) 67,182
   × 1,402
   —————

19)   16,173
     × 3,966

20)   16,327
     × 7,428

21)   97,220
     × 2,252

22)   87,084
     × 1,552

23)   59,408
     × 9,674

24)   50,217
     × 4,138

25)   22,740
     × 5,026

26)   55,230
     × 4,991

27)   33,075
     × 2,950

Multi Digit Decimals Multiplication

Find the product.

1)
$$
\begin{array}{r}
144.61 \\
\times\ \ 63.30 \\
\hline
\end{array}
$$

2)
$$
\begin{array}{r}
150.17 \\
\times\ \ 63.73 \\
\hline
\end{array}
$$

3)
$$
\begin{array}{r}
582.26 \\
\times\ \ 79.37 \\
\hline
\end{array}
$$

4)
$$
\begin{array}{r}
961.89 \\
\times\ \ 92.77 \\
\hline
\end{array}
$$

5)
$$
\begin{array}{r}
113.51 \\
\times\ \ 54.26 \\
\hline
\end{array}
$$

6)
$$
\begin{array}{r}
801.50 \\
\times\ \ 43.79 \\
\hline
\end{array}
$$

7)
$$
\begin{array}{r}
964.17 \\
\times\ \ 81.17 \\
\hline
\end{array}
$$

8)
$$
\begin{array}{r}
338.76 \\
\times\ \ 54.82 \\
\hline
\end{array}
$$

9)
$$
\begin{array}{r}
303.63 \\
\times\ \ 10.31 \\
\hline
\end{array}
$$

10)   617.08
 ×   52.62

11)   903.33
 ×   69.65

12)   302.53
 ×   29.64

13)   988.24
 ×   87.26

14)   147.06
 ×   36.53

15)   399.92
 ×   43.29

16)   637.53
 ×   51.44

17)   826.54
 ×   11.67

18)   541.17
 ×   25.70

19) 890.50 × 32.68	**20)** 392.51 × 61.02	**21)** 451.56 × 79.37
22) 893.35 × 35.07	**23)** 976.15 × 75.63	**24)** 117.11 × 35.12
25) 467.61 × 72.65	**26)** 376.52 × 59.76	**27)** 323.79 × 13.84

Dividing Decimals

Find the quotient.

1)

$7.2 \overline{)34.09}$

2)

$5.6 \overline{)53.66}$

3)

$6.5 \overline{)10.32}$

4)

$5.6 \overline{)16.25}$

5)

$5.4 \overline{)70.94}$

6)

$6.0 \overline{)24.68}$

7)

$8.3 \overline{)48.41}$

8)

$7.1 \overline{)79.06}$

9)

$2.2 \overline{)95.46}$

10)

$5.8 \overline{) 38.88}$

11)

$1.7 \overline{) 20.59}$

12)

$3.9 \overline{) 68.98}$

13)

$8.2 \overline{) 22.31}$

14)

$3.5 \overline{) 28.65}$

15)

$4.1 \overline{) 66.81}$

16)

$2.6 \overline{) 68.66}$

17)

$9.7 \overline{) 81.83}$

18)

$7.0 \overline{) 99.42}$

19)

$$5.4\overline{)28.03}$$

20)

$$8.9\overline{)53.41}$$

21)

$$4.0\overline{)63.27}$$

22)

$$7.0\overline{)47.12}$$

23)

$$8.3\overline{)52.22}$$

24)

$$2.0\overline{)54.17}$$

25)

$$1.1\overline{)66.72}$$

26)

$$6.0\overline{)83.90}$$

27)

$$5.1\overline{)76.86}$$

Place Value

Determine the place value of the underlined digit.

1) 718,374,186.7<u>6</u> = _______________________

2) 846,70<u>0</u>.20068 = _______________________

3) 37,050,<u>2</u>87.14 = _______________________

4) 16,735,05<u>0</u>,057 = _______________________

5) 846,722.6<u>6</u>838 = _______________________

6) 7,704,<u>7</u>76,240.8 = _______________________

7) 656,697,<u>3</u>15.98 = _______________________

8) 81,887,398.95<u>4</u> = ________________________________

9) 285,<u>5</u>78.89861 = ________________________________

10) 57,<u>3</u>40,573,266 = ________________________________

11) 906,5<u>7</u>6,770.26 = ________________________________

12) 89,30<u>2</u>,585,385 = ________________________________

13) 1,638,515,614.<u>3</u> = ________________________________

14) 2,199,783.<u>9</u>777 = ________________________________

15) 93,<u>1</u>90,402,678 = ________________________________

16) 56,642,326.0_7_3 = _______________________

17) 69,026,237.60_9_ = _______________________

18) 5,531,830.6_0_62 = _______________________

19) 546,35_7_.89983 = _______________________

20) 983,06_7_.722 = _______________________

21) _5_,286,396,918.4 = _______________________

22) 143,025,_2_30.17 = _______________________

23) 30,234,5_4_5.339 = _______________________

24) 672,724.93013 = _______________________________

25) 6,105,343,631 = _______________________________

26) 73,307,158,030 = _______________________________

27) 91,337,740,267 = _______________________________

28) 20,713,976.249 = _______________________________

29) 642,764,590.46 = _______________________________

30) 12,068,042.495 = _______________________________

Place Value and Expanded Notation

1) _________________________________   4 hundred millions + 5 ten millions + 3 millions + 5 hundred thousands + 7 ten thousands + 6 thousands + 4 hundreds + 5 tens + 5 ones

2) _________________________________   4 millions + 8 hundred thousands + 6 ten thousands + 5 thousands + 6 hundreds + 8 tens + 8 tenths + 2 hundredths

3) _________________________________   5 hundred thousands + 5 ten thousands + 9 thousands + 2 hundreds + 8 tens + 7 ones + 9 tenths + 2 hundredths + 2 thousandths

4) _______________________

9 hundred thousands + 4 ten thousands + 3 thousands + 7 hundreds + 9 tens + 2 ones + 4 tenths + 2 hundredths + 9 thousandths

5) _______________________

7 hundred thousands + 7 thousands + 1 hundred + 2 tens + 8 ones + 7 tenths + 9 hundredths + 6 thousandths

6) _______________________

3 ten millions + 4 hundred thousands + 4 ten thousands + 8 thousands + 8 hundreds + 5 tens + 1 one + 7 tenths

7) _______________________

2 hundred thousands + 3 ten thousands + 2 thousands + 7 hundreds + 8 tens + 1 one + 5 tenths + 5 hundredths + 9 thousandths

8) _______________________ 7 hundred thousands + 4 ten thousands + 2 thousands + 4 hundreds + 6 tens + 1 one + 9 tenths + 1 hundredth + 2 thousandths

9) _______________________ 2 hundred millions + 4 millions + 2 hundred thousands + 6 ten thousands + 6 thousands + 3 hundreds + 2 tens + 9 ones

10) _______________________ 6 ten millions + 7 millions + 9 hundred thousands + 5 ten thousands + 9 thousands + 8 hundreds + 2 tens + 2 ones + 3 tenths

11) _______________________ 2 hundred thousands + 3 ten thousands + 4 thousands + 2 hundreds + 9 tens + 5 ones + 7 tenths + 6 hundredths + 8 thousandths

12) _________________________________

6 hundred millions + 9 ten millions + 5 hundred thousands + 1 ten thousand + 1 hundred + 6 tens + 9 ones

13) _________________________________

8 millions + 6 hundred thousands + 4 thousands + 5 hundreds + 2 tens + 7 ones + 6 tenths + 8 hundredths

14) _________________________________

5 ten millions + 2 millions + 7 hundred thousands + 6 ten thousands + 5 thousands + 3 hundreds + 2 tens + 4 ones + 9 tenths

15) _________________________________

1 hundred million + 4 millions + 2 hundred thousands + 4 ten thousands + 5 thousands + 6 tens + 1 one

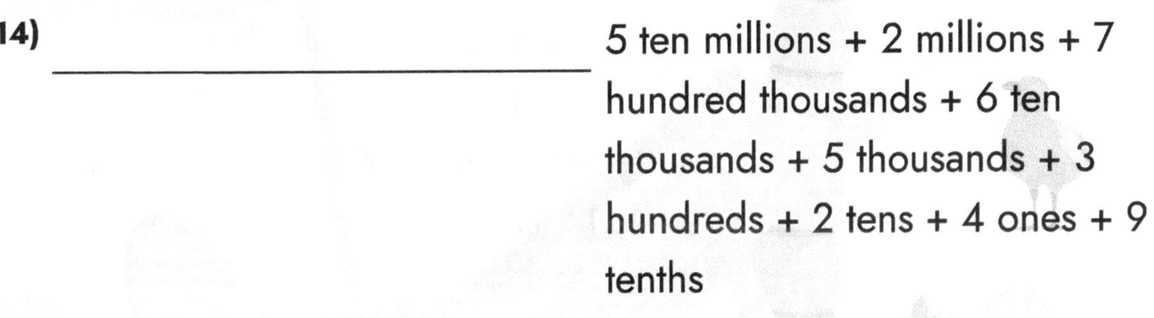
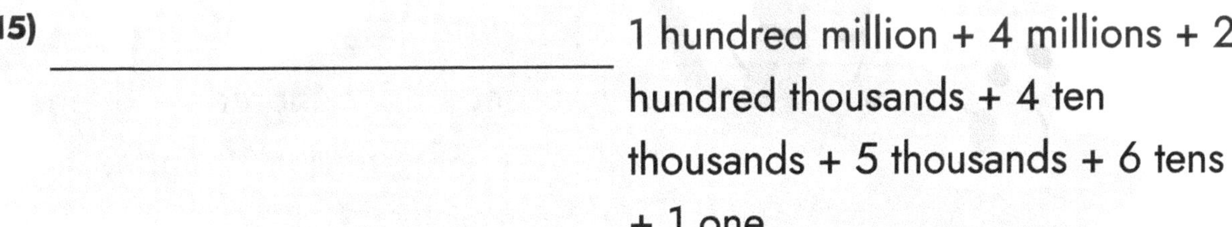

16) _______________________________

2 hundred millions + 5 ten millions + 1 million + 4 hundred thousands + 3 ten thousands + 6 thousands + 5 hundreds + 9 tens + 8 ones

17) _______________________________

5 hundred thousands + 7 ten thousands + 6 thousands + 8 hundreds + 9 tens + 4 ones + 7 tenths + 5 hundredths + 5 thousandths

18) _______________________________

3 ten millions + 1 million + 1 hundred thousand + 3 ten thousands + 6 thousands + 8 hundreds + 9 tens + 3 ones + 6 tenths

19) _______________________________

4 hundred thousands + 8 ten thousands + 7 hundreds + 3 tens + 2 ones + 8 tenths + 1 hundredth + 7 thousandths

Factors

1) 96 ____

2) 13 ____

3) 6 ____

4) 30 ____

5) 99 ____

6) 100 ____

7) 39 ____

8) 34 ___________________________

9) 35 ___________________________

10) 5 ___________________________

11) 7 ___________________________

12) 79 ___________________________

13) 31 ___________________________

14) 49 ___________________________

15) 8 ____

16) 17 ____

17) 3 ____

18) 88 ____

19) 16 ____

20) 90 ____

21) 54 ____

22) 69

23) 74

24) 52

25) 2

26) 42

27) 43

28) 61

Multiples

1) 29 ____

2) 8 ____

3) 79 ____

4) 92 ____

5) 67 ____

6) 44 ____

7) 97 ____

8) 71

9) 6

10) 7

11) 4

12) 18

13) 58

14) 22

15) 47 ____

16) 86 ____

17) 50 ____

18) 55 ____

19) 2 ____

20) 1 ____

21) 17 ____

22) 30

23) 21

24) 94

25) 53

26) 52

27) 25

28) 61

29) 60 ____

30) 87 ____

31) 23 ____

32) 48 ____

33) 56 ____

34) 91 ____

35) 76 ____

Convert Fractions and Decimals

Convert Fractions to Decimals and Decimals to Fractions.

1) $\dfrac{1}{3}$ = _______________

2) $\dfrac{10}{24}$ = _______________

3) $\dfrac{15}{36}$ = _______________

4) $\dfrac{468}{500}$ = _______________

5) 0.556 = _______________

6) $\dfrac{2}{19}$ = _______________

7) $\dfrac{19}{23}$ = _______________

8) $\dfrac{11}{40}$ = _______________

9) 0.45 = _______________

10) 0.278 = _______________

11) $\dfrac{4}{6}$ = _______________

12) $\dfrac{7}{50}$ = _______________

13) 0.4 = __________

14) $\frac{1}{14}$ = __________

15) $\frac{3}{10}$ = __________

16) 0.75 = __________

17) 0.455 = __________

18) 0.870 = __________

19) $\frac{1}{4}$ = __________

20) 0.778 = __________

21) $\frac{1}{2}$ = __________

22) 0.386 = __________

23) $\frac{5}{7}$ = __________

24) $\frac{12}{22}$ = __________

25) $\frac{1}{19} =$ ___________________

26) $0.481 =$ ___________________

27) $\frac{2}{60} =$ ___________________

28) $\frac{82}{100} =$ ___________________

29) $0.76 =$ ___________________

30) $\frac{14}{32} =$ ___________________

31) $\frac{19}{36} =$ ___________________

32) $0.5 =$ ___________________

33) $\frac{13}{17} =$ ___________________

34) $\frac{15}{16} =$ ___________________

35) $\frac{8}{12} =$ ___________________

36) $0.133 =$ ___________________

Mixed Numbers

1) $5\frac{1}{19} =$ _______________

2) $7\frac{7}{16} =$ _______________

3) $\frac{93}{11} =$ _______________

4) $4\frac{10}{12} =$ _______________

5) $\frac{77}{14} =$ _______________

6) $\frac{14}{5} =$ _______________

7) $3\frac{1}{8} =$ _______________

8) $1\frac{3}{17} =$ _______________

9) $2\frac{21}{28} =$ _______________

10) $8\frac{1}{2} =$ _______________

11) $8\frac{4}{20} =$ _______________

12) $3\frac{10}{14} =$ _______________

13) $2\frac{4}{38} =$ _______________

14) $3\frac{5}{36} =$ _______________

15) $\dfrac{290}{30} =$ ___________

16) $6\dfrac{3}{5} =$ ___________

17) $1\dfrac{10}{16} =$ ___________

18) $\dfrac{60}{14} =$ ___________

19) $8\dfrac{6}{12} =$ ___________

20) $3\dfrac{9}{14} =$ ___________

21) $\dfrac{248}{40} =$ ___________

22) $\dfrac{299}{30} =$ ___________

23) $2\dfrac{1}{18} =$ ___________

24) $\dfrac{97}{36} =$ ___________

25) $6\dfrac{3}{6} =$ ___________

26) $5\dfrac{4}{10} =$ ___________

27) $9\dfrac{1}{2} =$ ___________

28) $\dfrac{60}{18} =$ ___________

Mixed Numbers: Addition and Subtraction

Calculate.

1) $4\frac{6}{9} - 2\frac{1}{2} =$ _______________________

2) $7\frac{8}{9} - 3\frac{2}{8} =$ _______________________

3) $5\frac{3}{7} + 5\frac{3}{10} =$ _______________________

4) $6\frac{1}{6} - 1\frac{2}{4} =$ _______________________

5) $1\frac{1}{5} + 8\frac{2}{3} =$ _______________________

6) $8\frac{3}{7} + 8\frac{4}{6} =$ _______________________

7) $1\frac{2}{5} + 3\frac{2}{9} =$ ______________________

8) $8\frac{3}{4} - 7\frac{1}{2} =$ ______________________

9) $7\frac{2}{3} + 6\frac{9}{10} =$ ______________________

10) $6\frac{2}{8} - 3\frac{4}{9} =$ ______________________

11) $7\frac{2}{4} - 3\frac{3}{10} =$ ______________________

12) $4\frac{1}{5} - 2\frac{5}{6} =$ ______________________

13) $5\frac{6}{9} + 5\frac{2}{8} =$ ______________________

14) $3\frac{2}{3} + 5\frac{1}{2} =$ _______________________

15) $7\frac{2}{7} + 1\frac{5}{9} =$ _______________________

16) $9\frac{4}{5} - 8\frac{6}{10} =$ _______________________

17) $7\frac{3}{6} - 6\frac{1}{2} =$ _______________________

18) $3\frac{5}{8} + 3\frac{2}{4} =$ _______________________

19) $7\frac{2}{3} + 5\frac{2}{7} =$ _______________________

20) $1\frac{3}{4} + 4\frac{1}{7} =$ _______________________

21) $5 \frac{3}{8} - 3 \frac{2}{9} =$ _______________

22) $4 \frac{1}{3} - 1 \frac{1}{5} =$ _______________

23) $5 \frac{3}{6} - 1 \frac{5}{10} =$ _______________

24) $9 \frac{1}{2} - 8 \frac{2}{4} =$ _______________

25) $9 \frac{4}{7} - 7 \frac{4}{5} =$ _______________

26) $8 \frac{7}{10} + 3 \frac{2}{8} =$ _______________

Mixed Numbers: Multiplication and Division

Calculate.

1) $8\frac{1}{2} \times 2\frac{5}{7} =$ _______________________________

2) $7\frac{3}{8} \div 6\frac{3}{9} =$ _______________________________

3) $2\frac{1}{3} \times 3\frac{4}{6} =$ _______________________________

4) $4\frac{5}{9} \times 7\frac{1}{4} =$ _______________________________

5) $9\frac{5}{7} \times 3\frac{1}{2} =$ _______________________________

6) $7\frac{5}{8} \times 1\frac{8}{10} =$ _______________________________

7) $2\frac{2}{5} \div 4\frac{4}{9} =$ _______________________

8) $7\frac{2}{8} \times 1\frac{1}{4} =$ _______________________

9) $6\frac{1}{2} \div 2\frac{6}{7} =$ _______________________

10) $9\frac{2}{5} \times 7\frac{1}{3} =$ _______________________

11) $1\frac{4}{10} \times 3\frac{4}{6} =$ _______________________

12) $7\frac{2}{3} \times 7\frac{1}{2} =$ _______________________

13) $1\frac{3}{4} \times 4\frac{3}{5} =$ _______________________

14) $5\frac{4}{9} \times 9\frac{7}{10} =$ _______________________

15) $5\frac{4}{7} \times 6\frac{3}{8} =$ _______________________

16) $2\frac{3}{6} \div 9\frac{1}{9} =$ _______________________

17) $1\frac{1}{8} \times 2\frac{2}{5} =$ _______________________

18) $4\frac{3}{10} \times 7\frac{1}{3} =$ _______________________

19) $8\frac{1}{2} \div 3\frac{3}{6} =$ _______________________

20) $7\frac{1}{7} \div 9\frac{2}{4} =$ _______________________

21) $5\frac{3}{9} \times 3\frac{3}{7} =$ ___________

22) $3\frac{2}{4} \times 5\frac{7}{10} =$ ___________

23) $6\frac{1}{3} \div 5\frac{2}{6} =$ ___________

24) $2\frac{2}{8} \div 2\frac{1}{2} =$ ___________

25) $6\frac{3}{5} \div 3\frac{2}{4} =$ ___________

26) $6\frac{4}{5} \times 7\frac{3}{9} =$ ___________

Multiplication with Whole Numbers

1) $\frac{8}{14}$ of 8 = _______________

2) $\frac{2}{8}$ of 1 = _______________

3) $\frac{1}{2}$ of 5 = _______________

4) $\frac{10}{12}$ of 9 = _______________

5) $8 \times \frac{4}{17}$ = _______________

6) $4 \times \frac{7}{10}$ = _______________

7) $4 \times \frac{5}{7}$ = _______________

8) $7 \times \frac{1}{9}$ = _______________

9) $\frac{12}{19}$ of 8 = _______________

10) $\frac{2}{6}$ of 6 = _______________

11) $5 \times \frac{15}{20}$ = _______________

12) $6 \times \frac{1}{2}$ = _______________

13) $5 \times \frac{3}{12}$ = _______________

14) $8 \times \frac{2}{4}$ = _______________

15) $3 \times \dfrac{2}{14} =$ _______________

16) $\dfrac{1}{3}$ of $4 =$ _______________

17) $\dfrac{1}{10}$ of $8 =$ _______________

18) $\dfrac{1}{6}$ of $9 =$ _______________

19) $\dfrac{2}{13}$ of $5 =$ _______________

20) $\dfrac{2}{8}$ of $6 =$ _______________

21) $\dfrac{9}{15}$ of $3 =$ _______________

22) $1 \times \dfrac{2}{7} =$ _______________

23) $\dfrac{14}{20}$ of $8 =$ _______________

24) $\dfrac{13}{16}$ of $5 =$ _______________

25) $3 \times \dfrac{16}{17} =$ _______________

26) $9 \times \dfrac{1}{11} =$ _______________

27) $\dfrac{4}{5}$ of $2 =$ _______________

28) $\dfrac{18}{19}$ of $3 =$ _______________

Simplify Fractions: Proper and Improper Fractions

1) $\dfrac{462}{66} =$ _______________

2) $\dfrac{63}{135} =$ _______________

3) $\dfrac{88}{12} =$ _______________

4) $\dfrac{540}{108} =$ _______________

5) $\dfrac{192}{66} =$ _______________

6) $\dfrac{105}{12} =$ _______________

7) $\dfrac{402}{108} =$ _______________

8) $\dfrac{64}{12} =$ _______________

9) $\dfrac{7}{49} =$ _______________

10) $\dfrac{26}{4} =$ _______________

11) $\dfrac{30}{50} =$ _______________

12) $\dfrac{16}{40} =$ _______________

13) $\dfrac{366}{38} =$ _______________

14) $\dfrac{50}{80} =$ _______________

15) $\dfrac{945}{119} =$ _________________

16) $\dfrac{135}{27} =$ _________________

17) $\dfrac{450}{90} =$ _________________

18) $\dfrac{58}{28} =$ _________________

19) $\dfrac{84}{16} =$ _________________

20) $\dfrac{70}{91} =$ _________________

21) $\dfrac{6}{120} =$ _________________

22) $\dfrac{12}{108} =$ _________________

23) $\dfrac{270}{90} =$ _________________

24) $\dfrac{693}{99} =$ _________________

25) $\dfrac{168}{42} =$ _________________

26) $\dfrac{18}{40} =$ _________________

27) $\dfrac{896}{112} =$ _________________

28) $\dfrac{36}{18} =$ _________________

29) $\dfrac{864}{144} =$ ___________________

30) $\dfrac{60}{12} =$ ___________________

31) $\dfrac{360}{72} =$ ___________________

32) $\dfrac{45}{153} =$ ___________________

33) $\dfrac{90}{45} =$ ___________________

34) $\dfrac{624}{78} =$ ___________________

35) $\dfrac{3}{18} =$ ___________________

36) $\dfrac{245}{70} =$ ___________________

37) $\dfrac{352}{36} =$ ___________________

38) $\dfrac{1044}{114} =$ ___________________

39) $\dfrac{228}{48} =$ ___________________

40) $\dfrac{234}{36} =$ ___________________

41) $\dfrac{350}{70} =$ ___________________

42) $\dfrac{66}{72} =$ ___________________

Area and Perimeter

1)

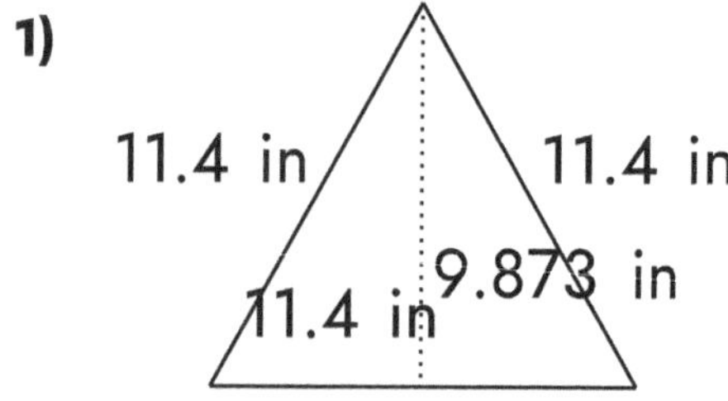

2)

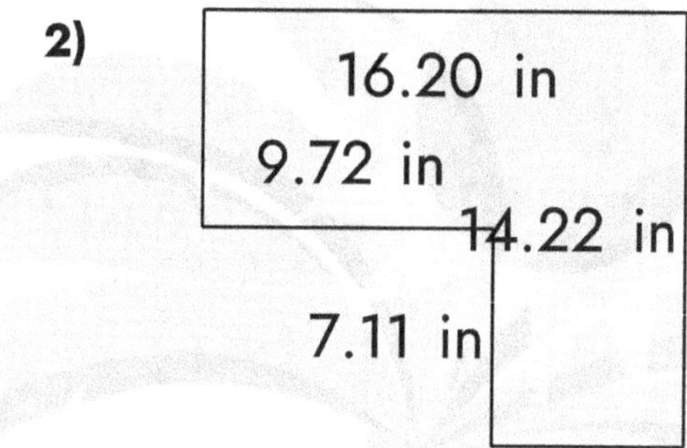

3)

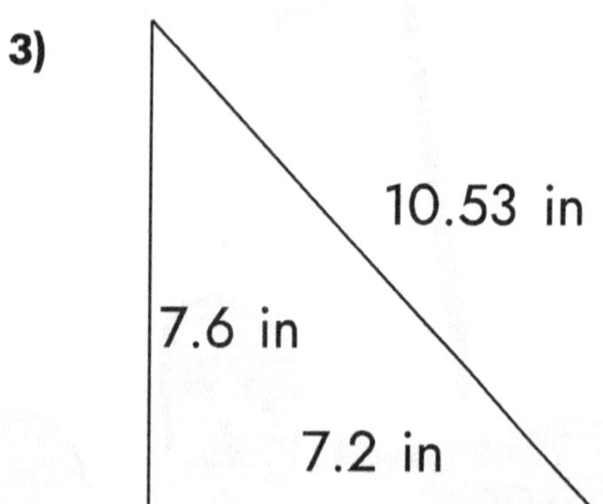

4)

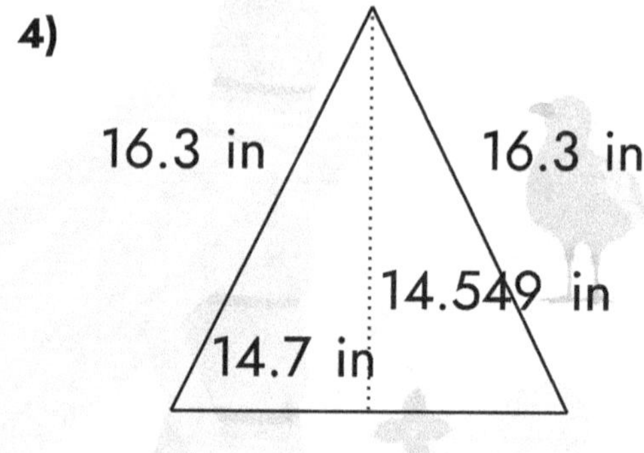

SUMMER MATH WORKBOOK
NAME:
BUILDING ACTIVITIES

5)

8.5 cm
8.8 cm
8.40 cm
4.1 cm

6)

8.2 cm
8.2 cm
7.528 cm
6.5 cm

7)

14.32 in
15.92 in

8)

7.12.92 cm
12.16 cm
8.48 cm

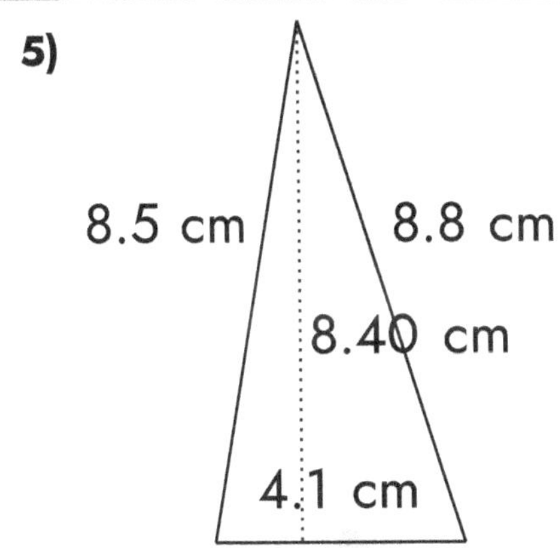

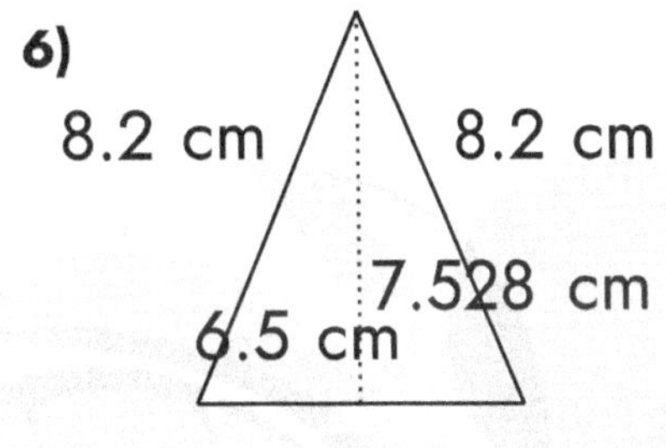

SUMMER MATH WORKBOOK
NAME:
BUILDING ACTIVITIES

9)

10.4 cm
10.4 cm
9.007 cm
10.4 cm

10)

9.84 cm
6.90 cm
9.24 cm
3.72 cm

11)

4.62 in
11.55 in
4.34 in
10.92 in

12)

12.40 in
10.3 in
6.9 in

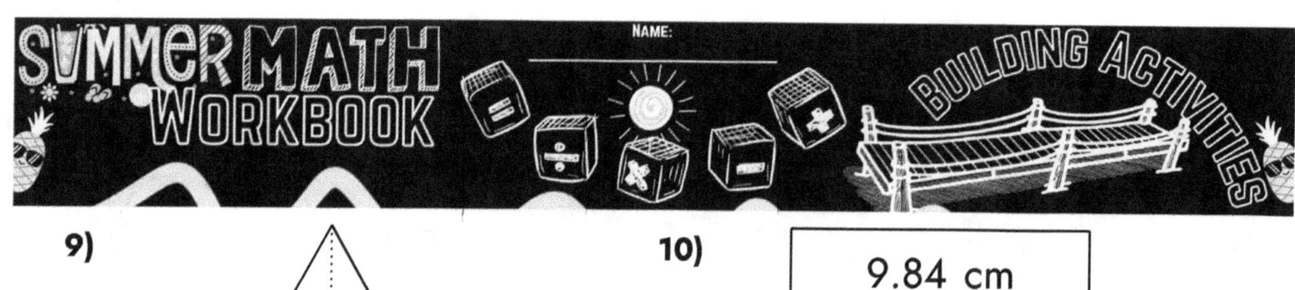

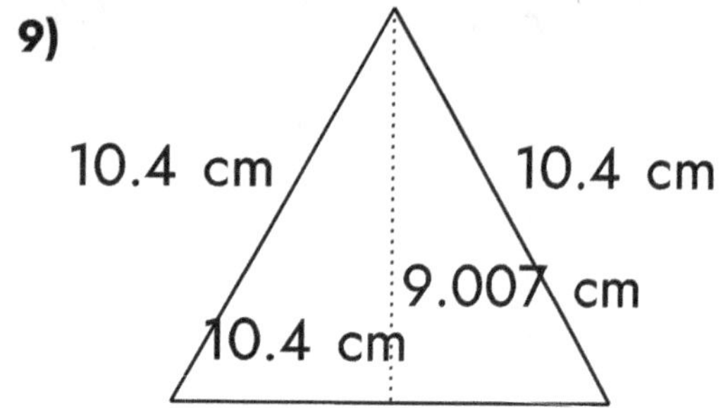

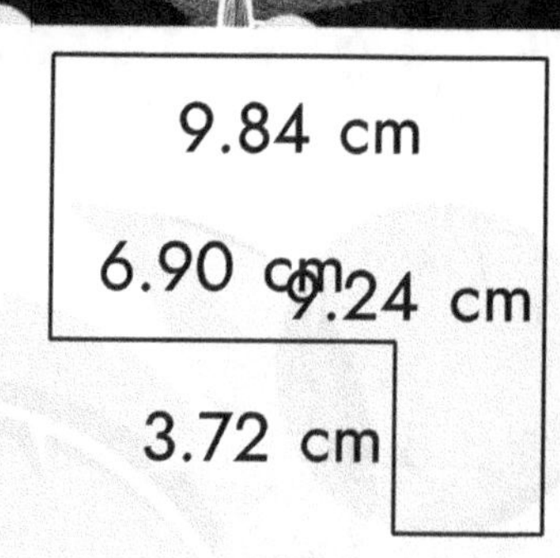

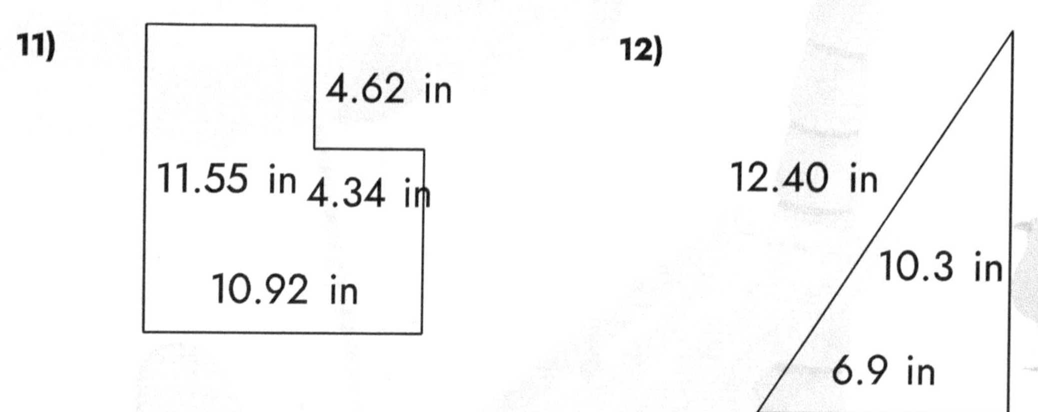

SUMMER MATH WORKBOOK
NAME:
BUILDING ACTIVITIES

13)

16.4 cm
15.5 cm
15.44 cm
7.4 cm

14)

6.1 in
6.1 in
5.586 in
4.9 in

15)

11.20 cm
11.12 cm

16)

14.49 in
4.32 in
17.55 in
12.24 in

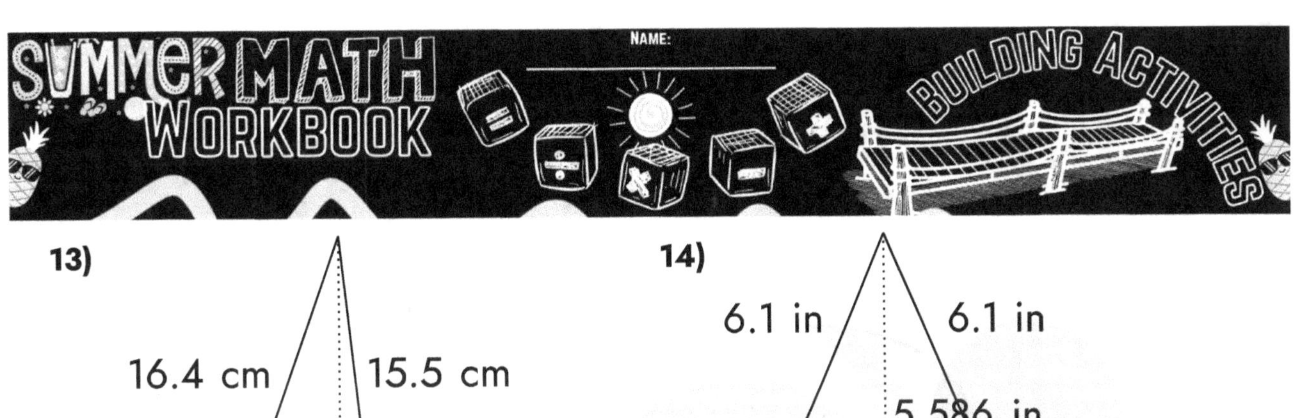

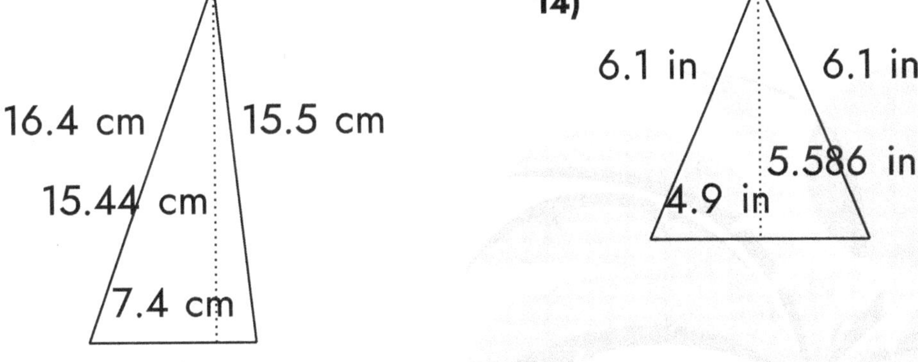

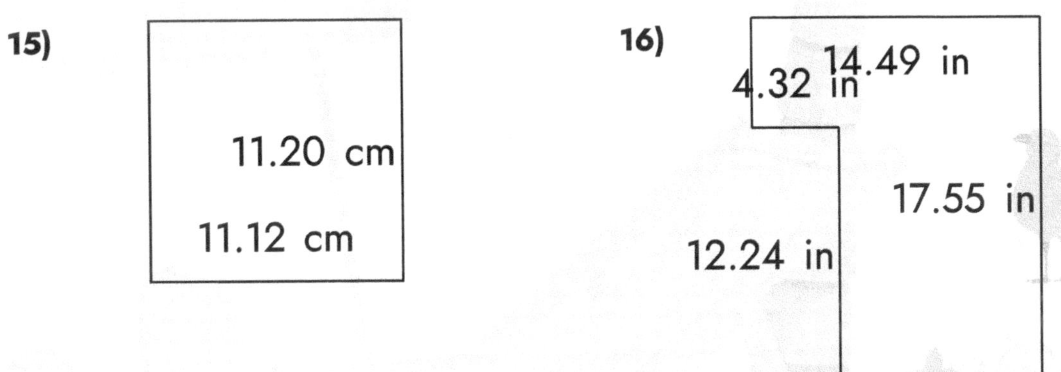

17)

16.00 cm

15.52 cm

18) 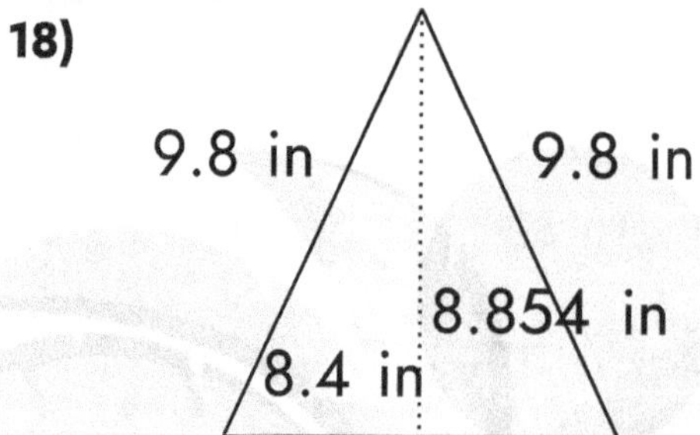

19) 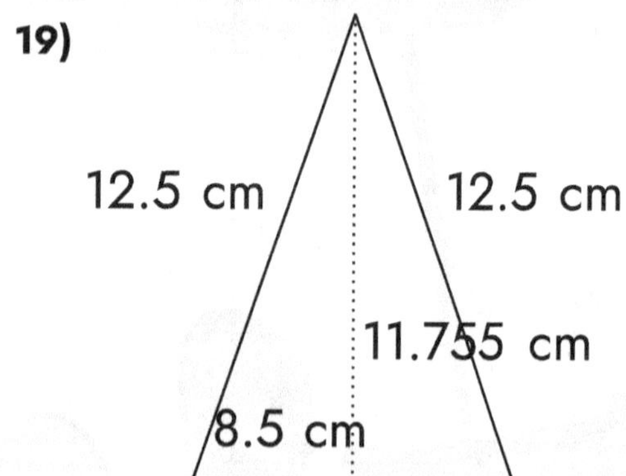

20) 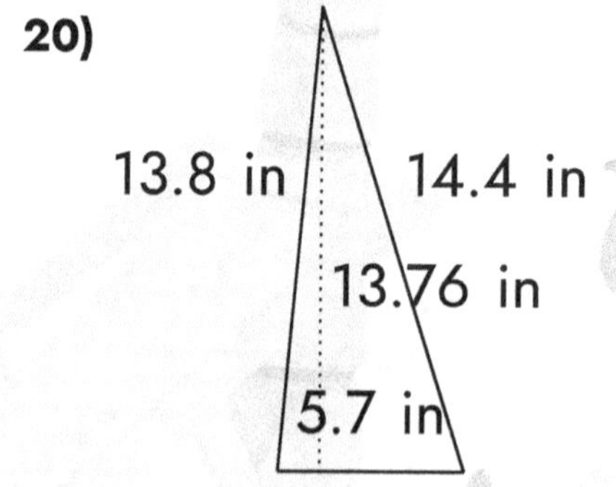

SUMMER MATH WORKBOOK
NAME:
BUILDING ACTIVITIES

21)

9.27 in
15.39 in
11.97 in
17.10 in

22)

18.84 in
13.6 in
13.0 in

23)

5.3 cm
7.2 cm
4.35 cm
8.7 cm

24)

7.50 cm
9.40 cm

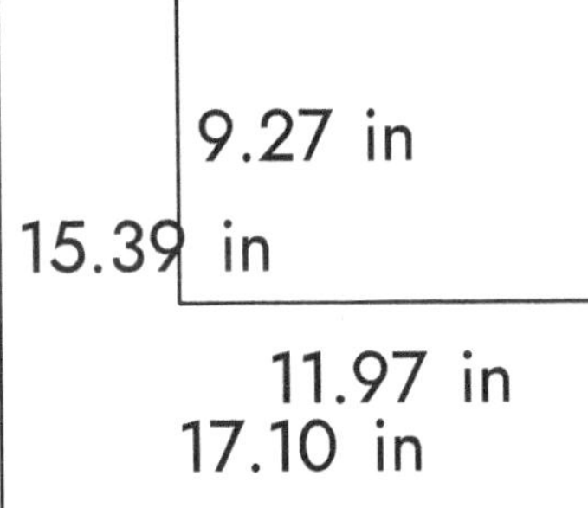

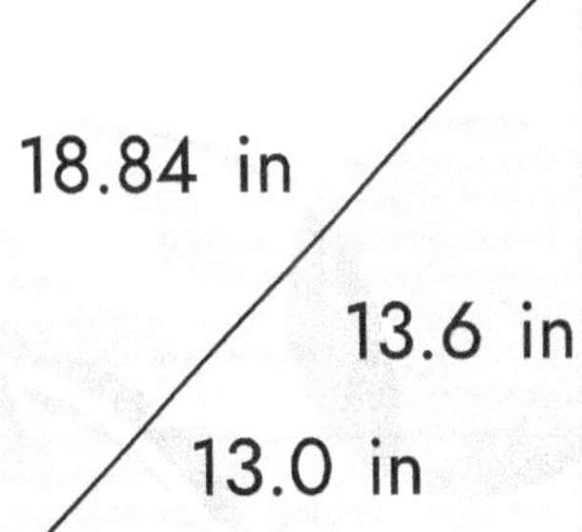

25)

16.08 in

11.0 in

11.8 in

26)

8.0 cm   8.0 cm

7.436 cm

5.9 cm

27)

9.06 in

8.70 in

28)

19.61 in

13.4 in

14.4 in

Area and Circumference

Calculate the circumference of each circle. Pi Value = 3.14

1)

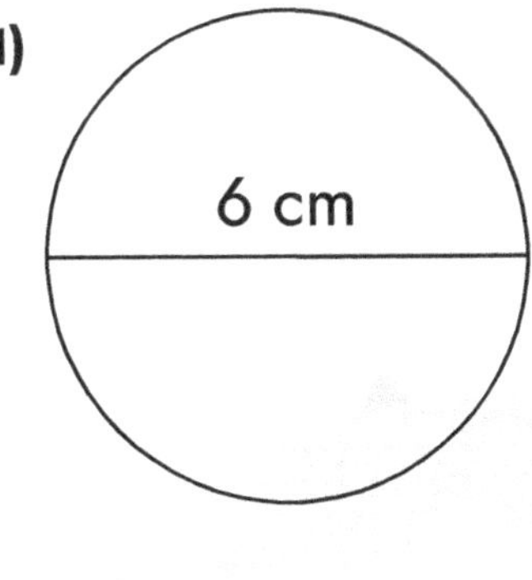

____

____

2)

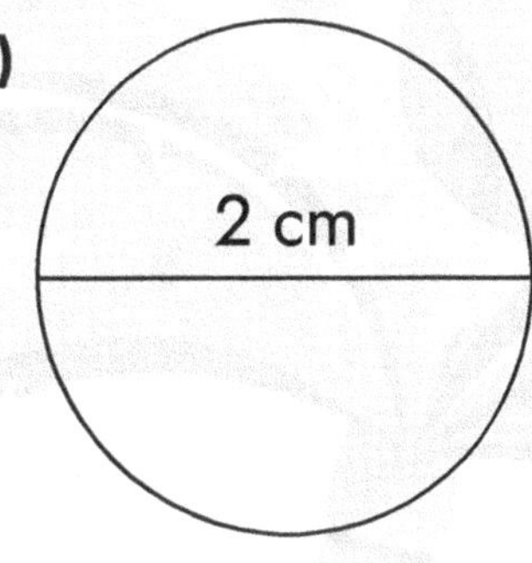

____

____

3)

____

____

4)

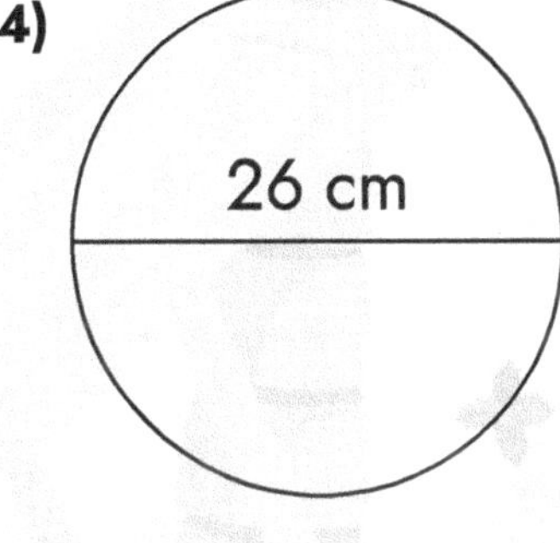

____

____

5)

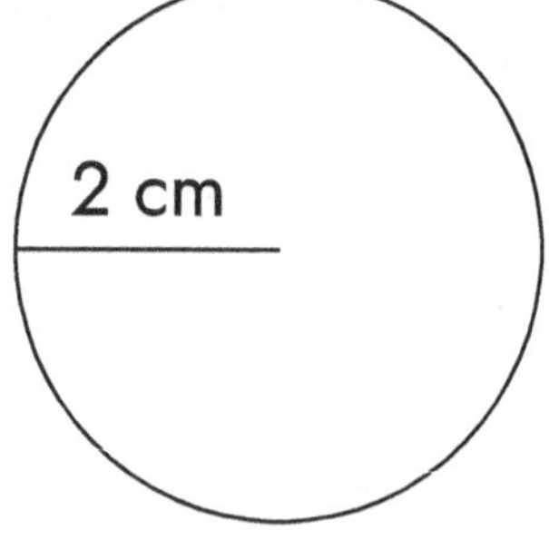

____

____

6)

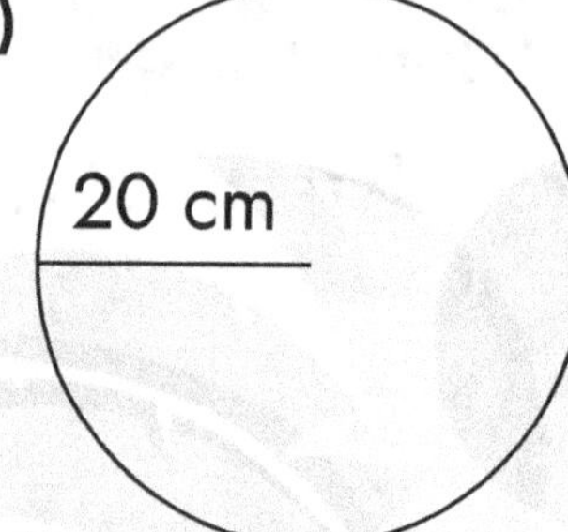

____

____

7)

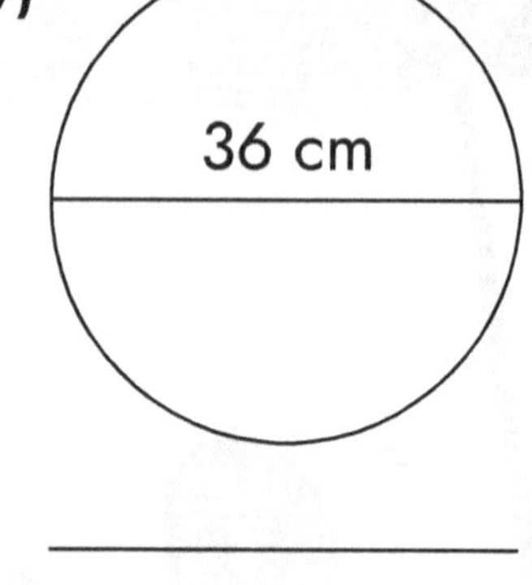

____

____

8)

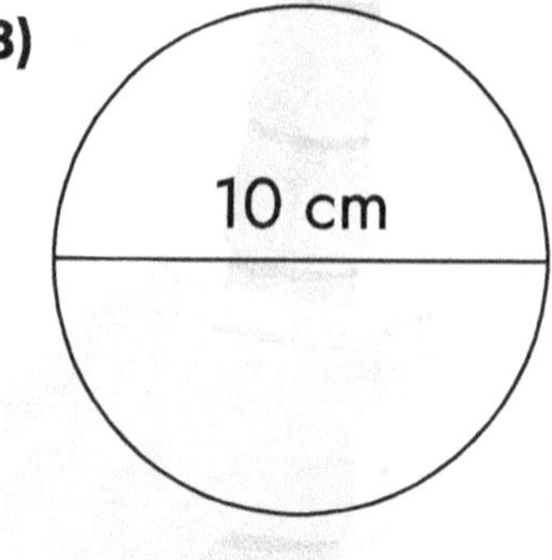

____

____

9)

12 cm

____

____

10)

38 cm

____

____

11)

11 cm

____

____

12)

34 cm

____

____

13)

7 cm

____

____

14)

4 cm

____

____

15)

24 cm

____

____

16)

15 cm

____

____

17)

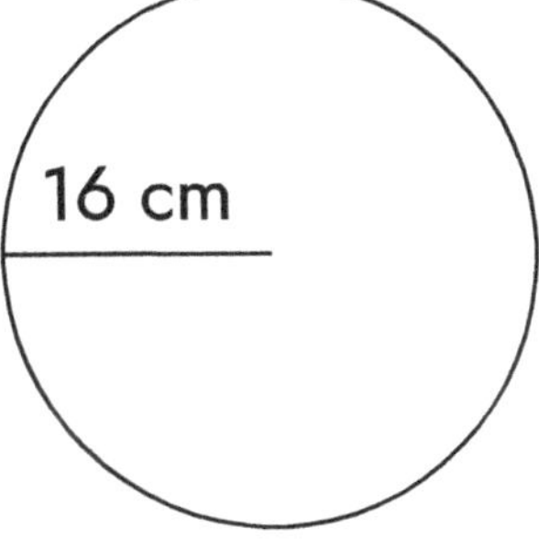

____

____

18)

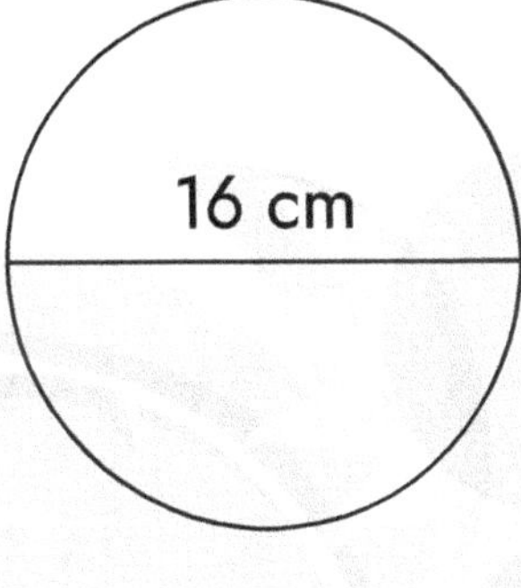

____

19)

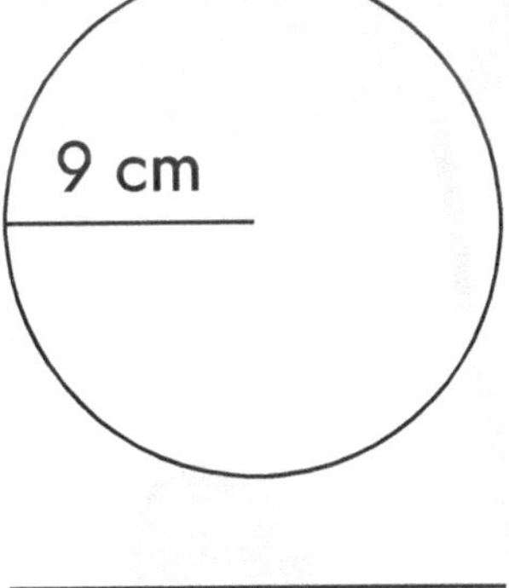

____

____

20)

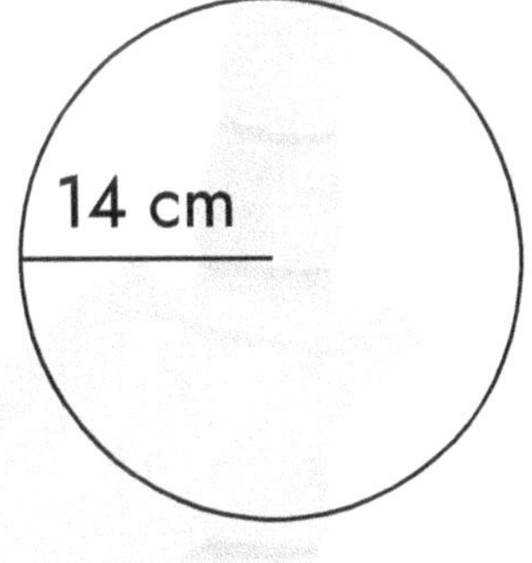

____

____

SUMMER MATH WORKBOOK
NAME:
BUILDING ACTIVITIES

21)

15 cm

____

____

22)

2 cm

____

____

23)

40 cm

____

____

24)

9 cm

____

____

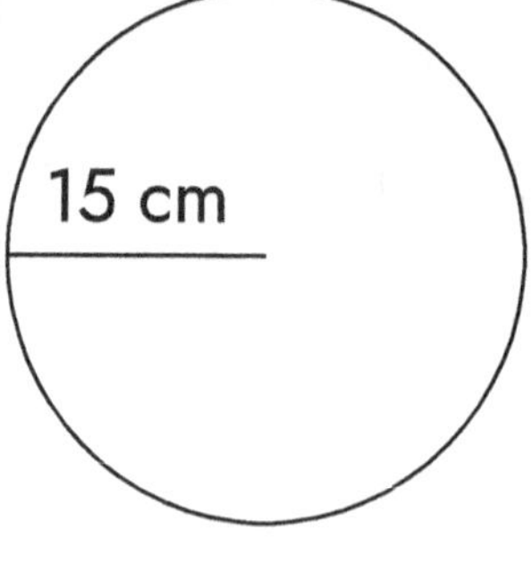

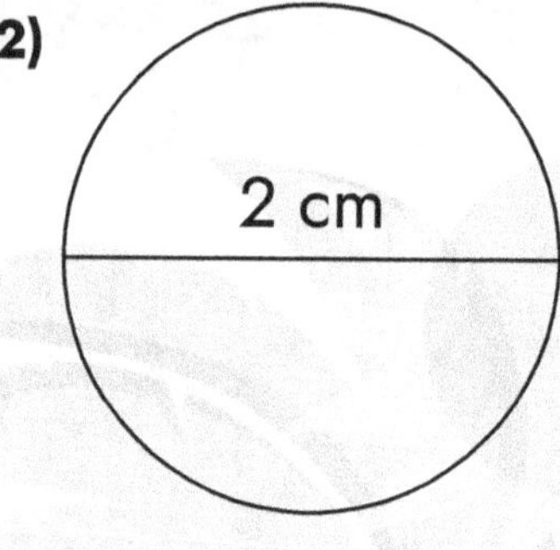

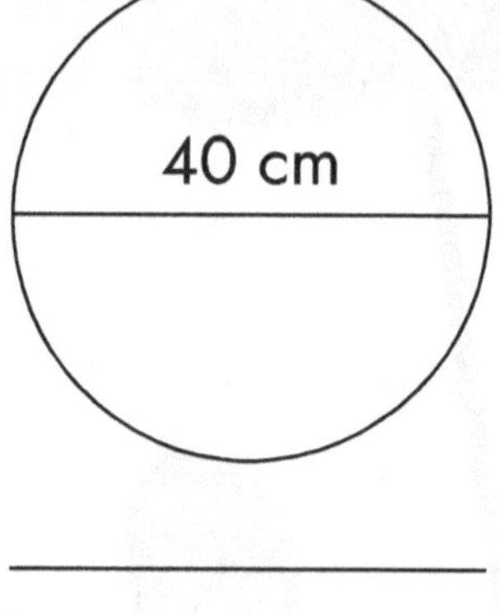

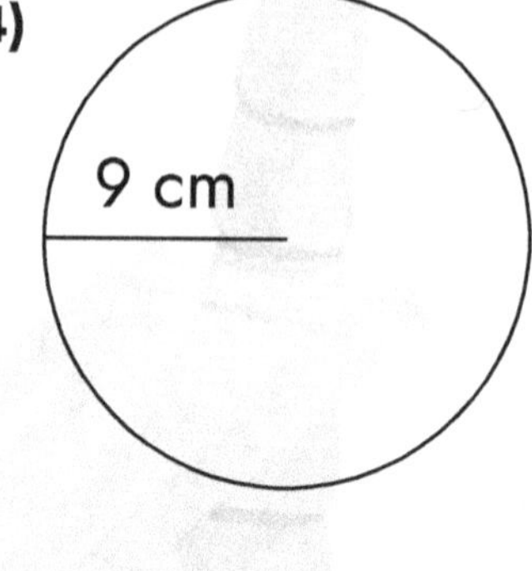

SUMMER MATH WORKBOOK
NAME:
BUILDING ACTIVITIES

25)

26 cm

____

____

26)

8 cm

____

____

27)

36 cm

____

____

28)

18 cm

____

____

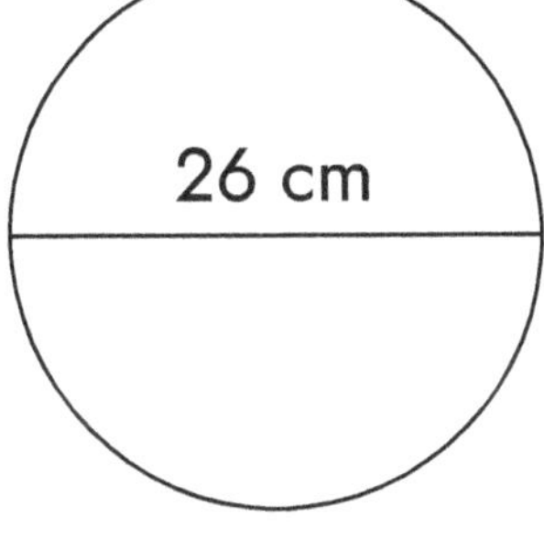

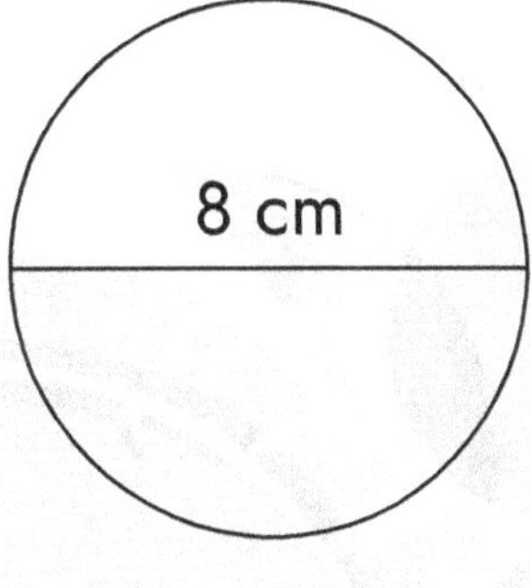

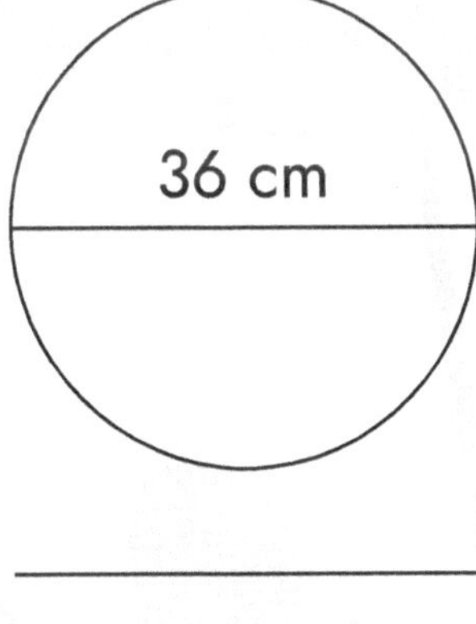

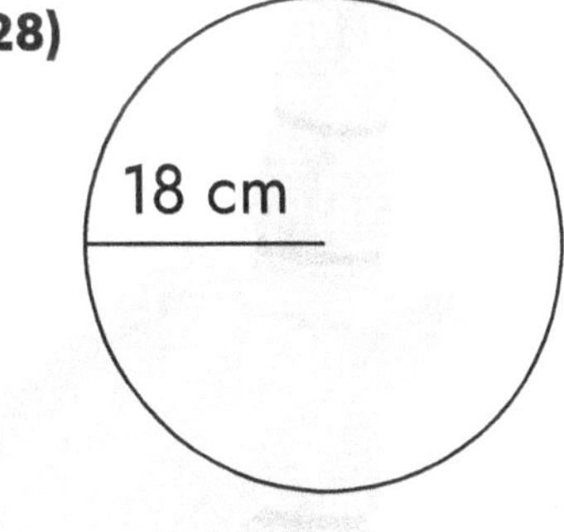

Measuring Angles

1)

____

2)

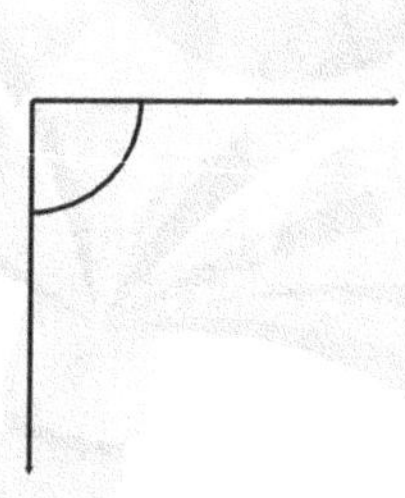

____

3)

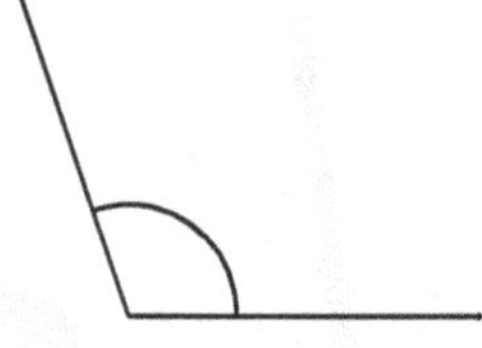

____

4)

____

5)

6)

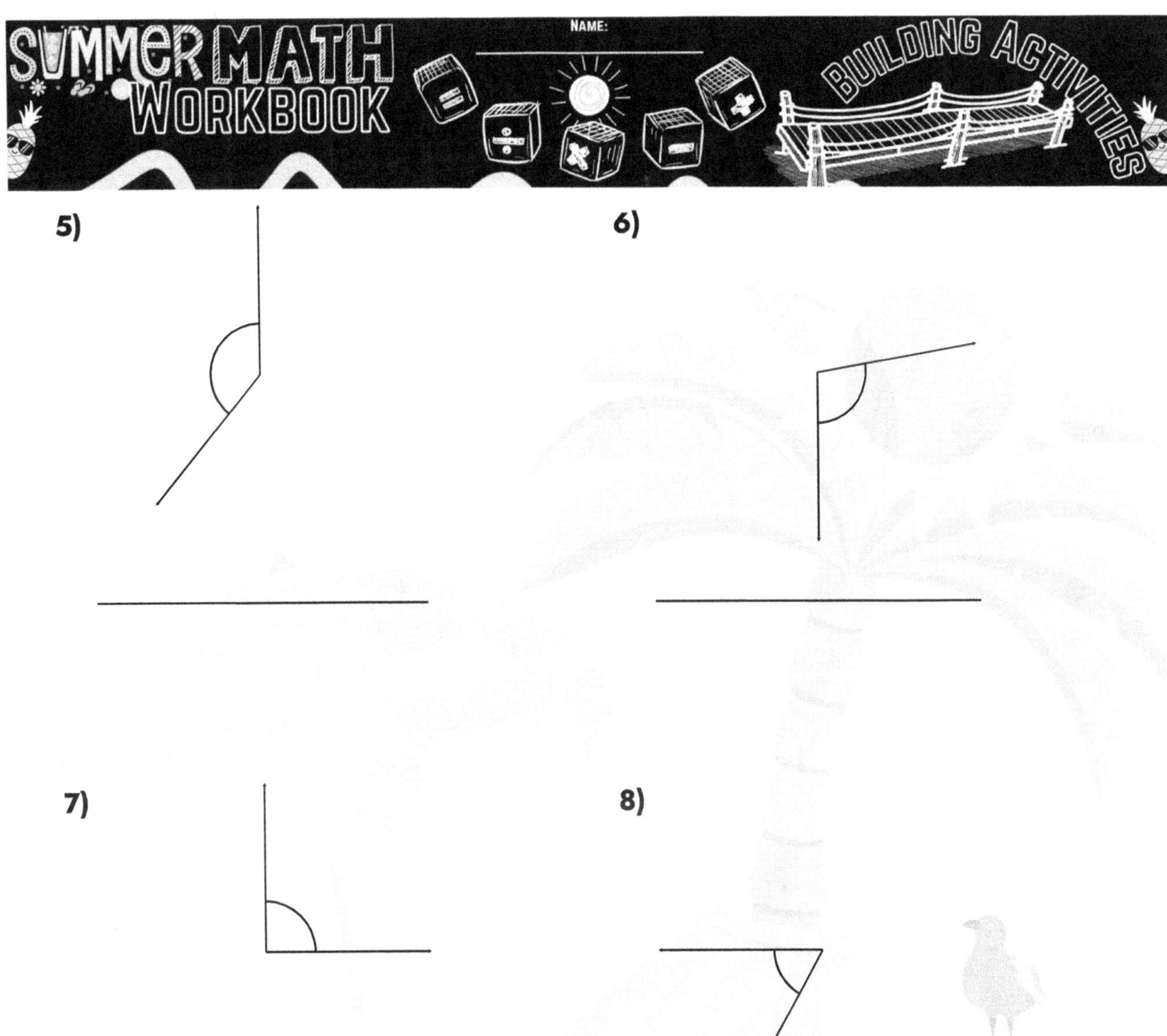

7)

8)

9)

____

10)

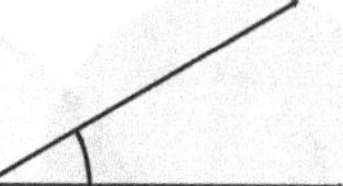

____

11)

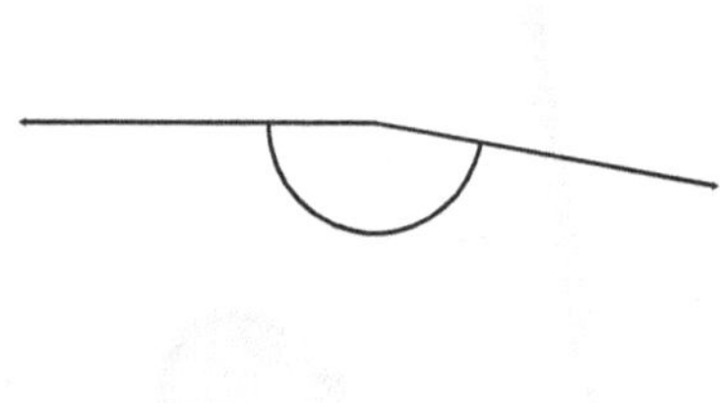

____

12)

____

13)

14)

15)

16)

17)

18)

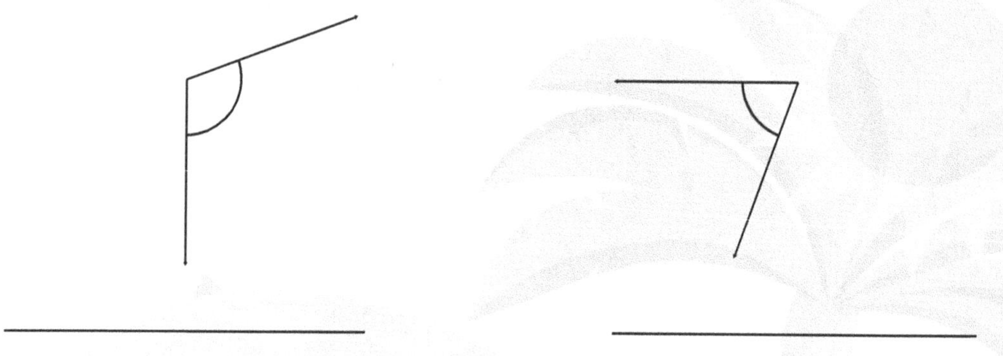

19)

20)

Volume and Surface Area

1)

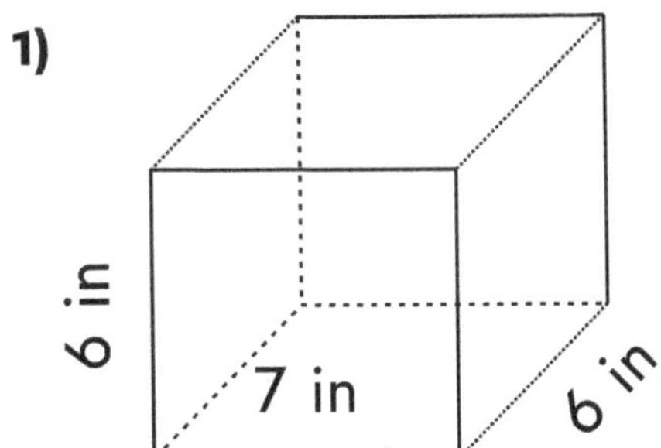

2)

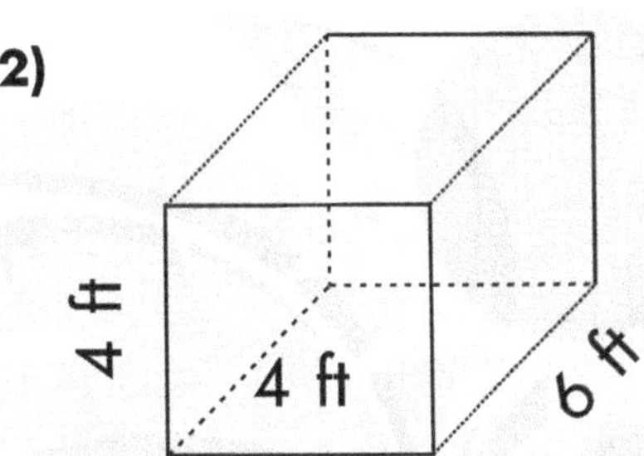

3)

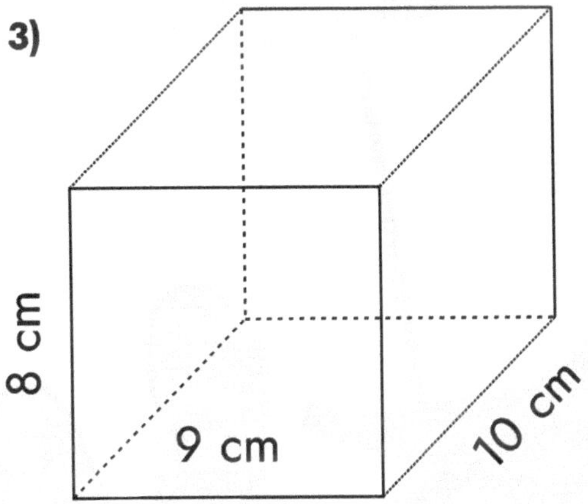

4)

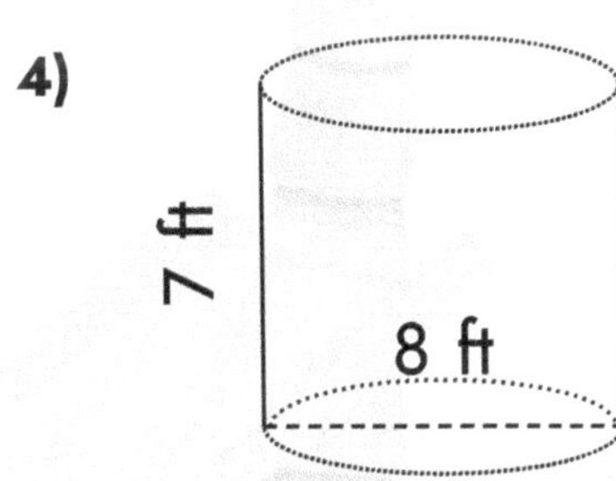

5)

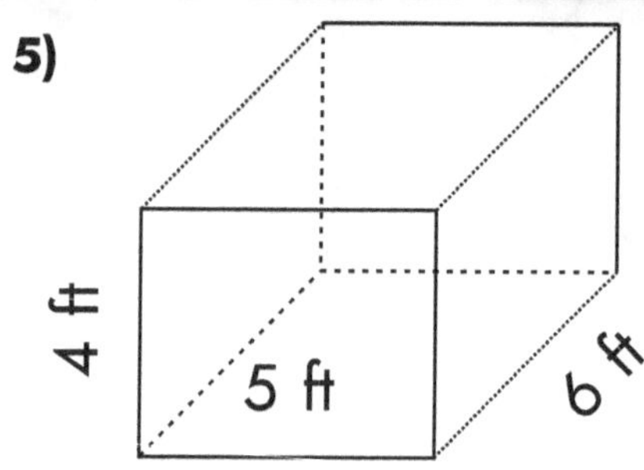

6)

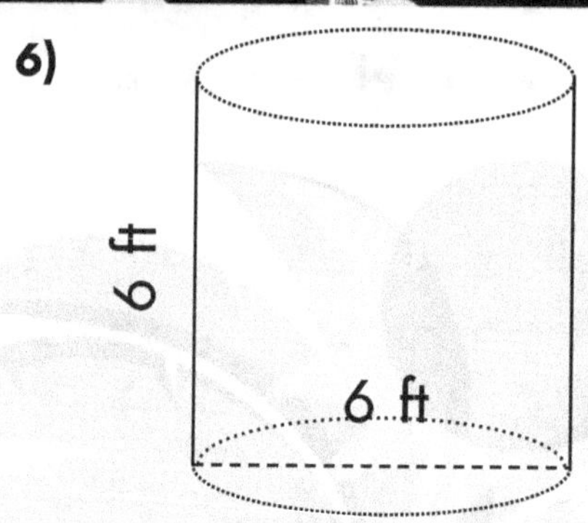

7)

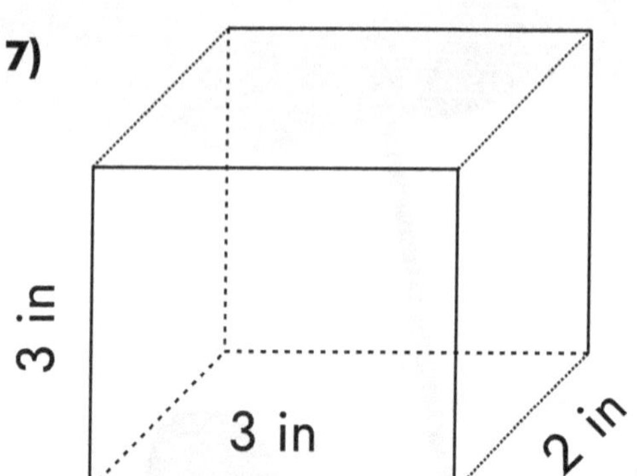

8)

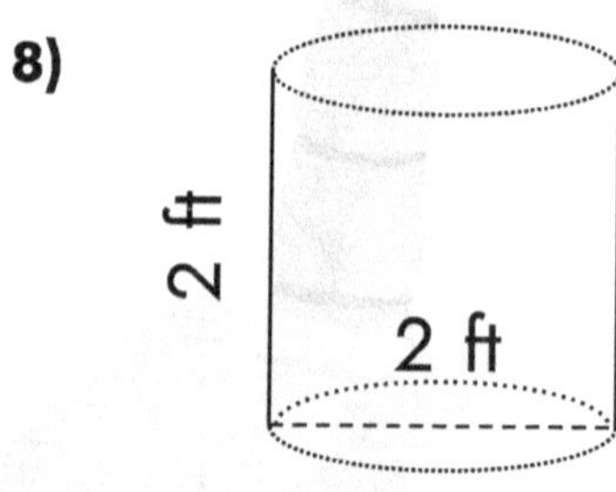

9)

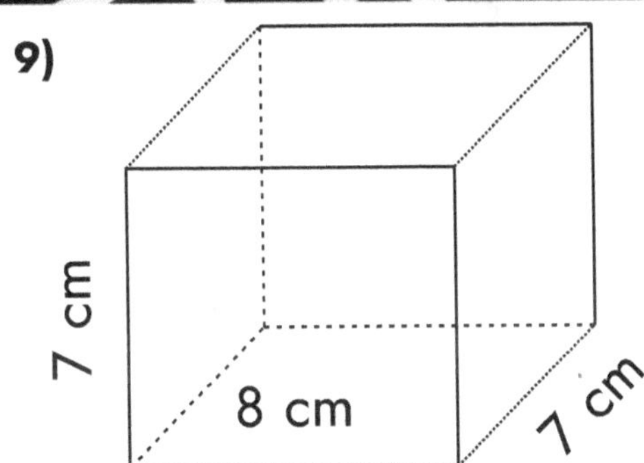

10)

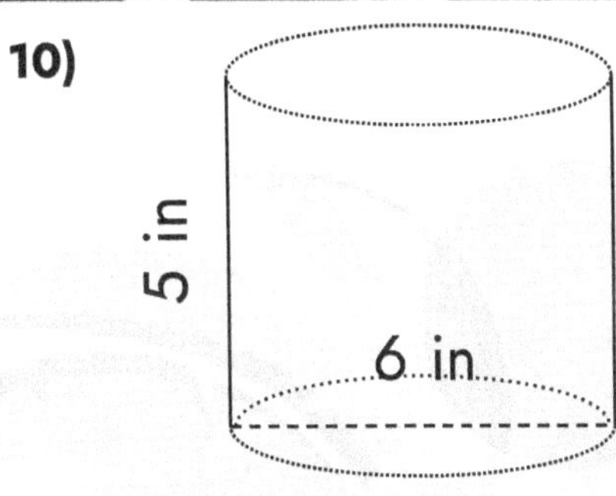

11)

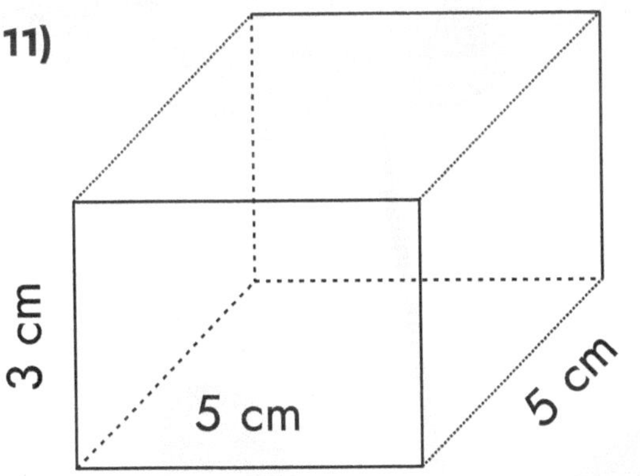

12)

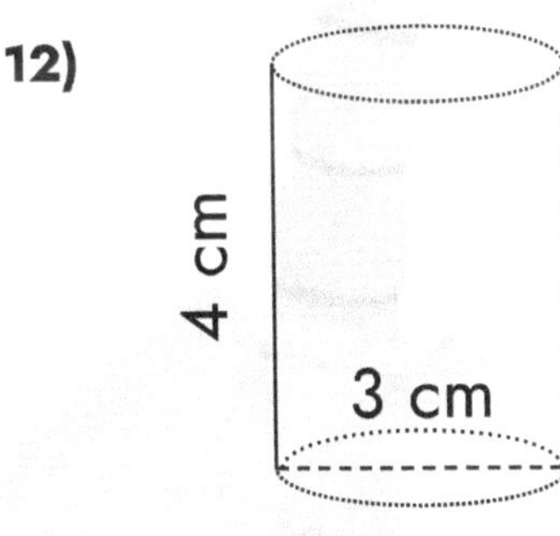

13)

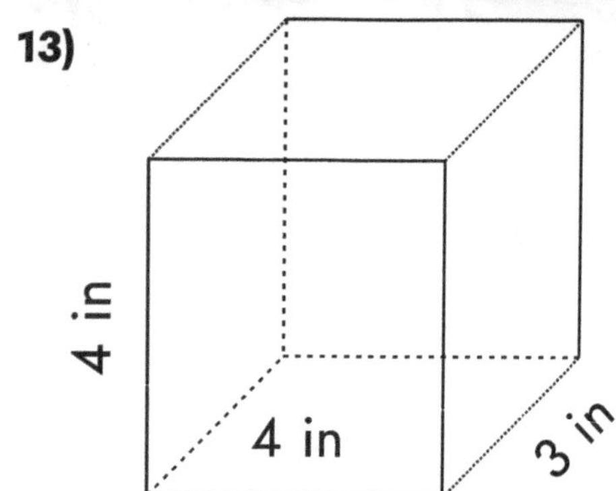

14)

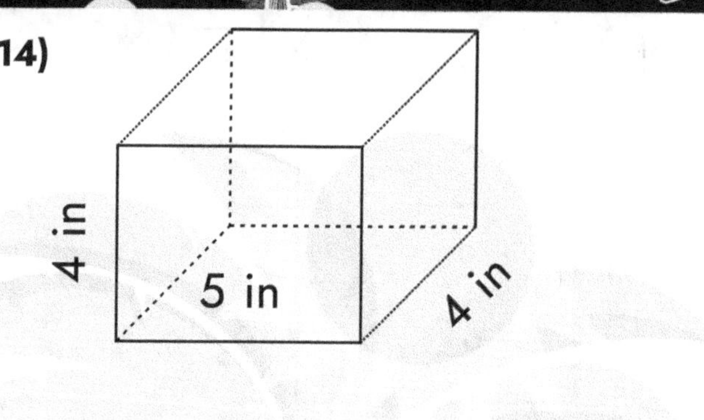

15)

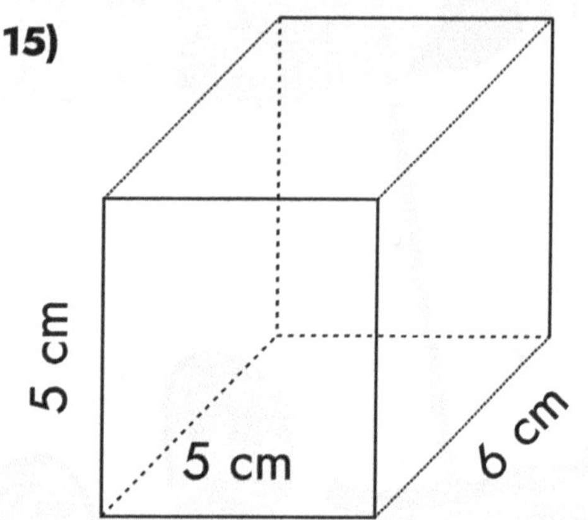

16)

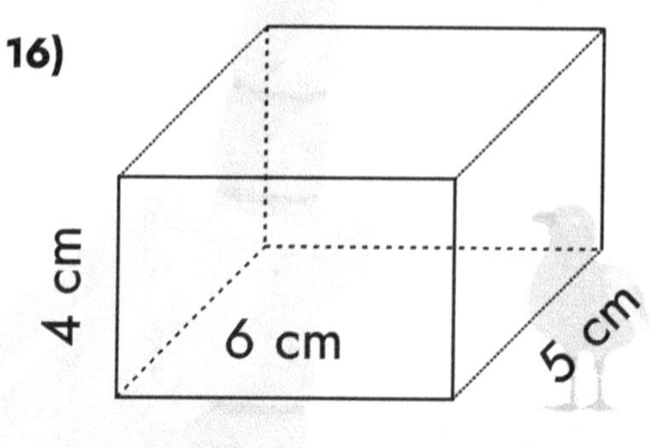

SUMMER MATH WORKBOOK
NAME:
BUILDING ACTIVITIES

17)

10 in
6 in

18)

6 in
6 in
6 in

19)

4 in
5 in
3 in

20)

6 in
5 in
7 in

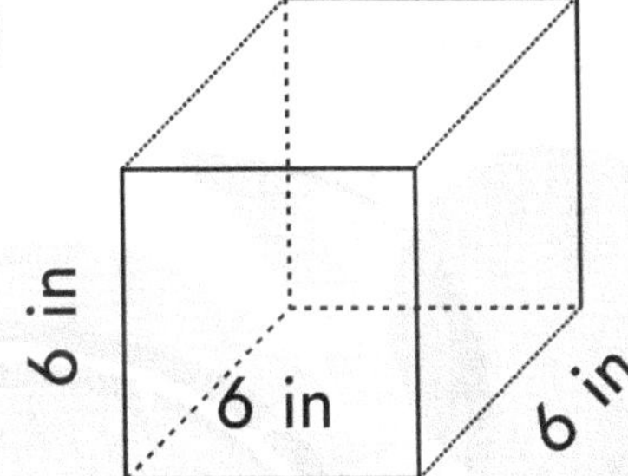

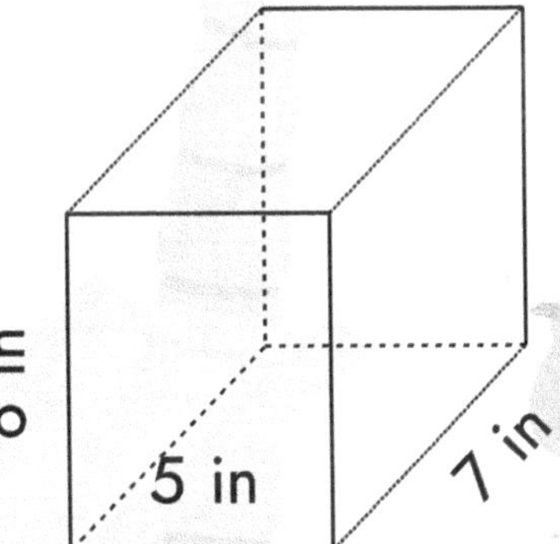

Metric Weights and Measures

Convert the given measures to new units.

1) 46 m = _______________ km

2) 25 m = _______________ km

3) 39 kL = _______________ L

4) 60 kL = _______________ L

5) 82 L = _______________ kL

6) 21 kL = _______________ L

7) 13 L = _______________ kL

8) 19 m = _______________ km

9) 62 kL = _______________ L

10) 33 t = _______________ kg

11) 77 kL = _______________ L

12) 60 kg = _______________ t

13) 97 t = _______________ kg

14) 36 L = _______________ kL

15) 80 kL = _________________ L

16) 53 km = _________________ m

17) 85 m = _________________ km

18) 52 L = _________________ kL

19) 90 kL = _________________ L

20) 55 kL = _________________ L

21) 62 km = _________________ m

22) 63 kL = _________________ L

23) 29 L = _________________ kL

24) 33 km = _________________ m

25) 11 km = _________________ m

26) 12 kg = _________________ t

27) 48 m = _________________ km

28) 10 t = _________________ kg

29) 42 km = _________________ m

30) 71 t = _________________ kg

Mean and Median

Find the Mean, Median of the following sets of data.

1) 22, 76, 88, 89, 25, 84

   Mean = _____   Median = _____

2) 12, 30, 67, 5, 95, 87

   Mean = _____   Median = _____

3) 88, 50, 14, 11, 61, 18

   Mean = _____   Median = _____

4) 52, 7, 78, 62, 98, 83

   Mean = _____   Median = _____

5) 57, 11, 30, 79, 10, 61

Mean = _______ Median = _____

6) 9, 60, 89, 7, 35, 22

Mean = _____ Median = _____

7) 41, 89, 24, 99, 36, 18

Mean = _______ Median = _____

8) 23, 46, 63, 73, 33, 75

Mean = _______ Median = _____

9) 86, 92, 81, 82, 46, 30

Mean = _____ Median = _____

10) 90, 59, 78, 6, 32, 14

Mean = _____   Median = _____

11) 54, 32, 21, 7, 95, 35

Mean = _______   Median = _____

12) 97, 81, 16, 92, 70, 72

Mean = _______   Median = _____

13) 93, 52, 70, 61, 39, 52

Mean = _______   Median = _____

14) 20, 84, 77, 55, 93, 18

Mean = _______   Median = _____

15) 79, 27, 15, 60, 17, 75

Mean = _____ Median = _____

16) 43, 35, 58, 10, 45, 5

Mean = _____ Median = _____

17) 97, 17, 50, 28, 75, 52

Mean = _____ Median = _____

18) 60, 94, 22, 10, 88, 93

Mean = _____ Median = _____

19) 60, 29, 21, 27, 85, 47

Mean = _____ Median = _____

20) 37, 99, 39, 3, 27, 69

Mean = _______   Median = _____

21) 21, 38, 65, 40, 50, 35

Mean = _____   Median = _____

22) 14, 84, 8, 65, 64, 23

Mean = _____   Median = _____

23) 2, 92, 10, 26, 95, 98

Mean = _______   Median = _____

24) 95, 70, 38, 21, 99, 87

Mean = _______   Median = _____

ANSWERS

Page 1:   Long Division: Remainders

1. 3,133 R3   **2.** 805 R4   **3.** 4,891 R4   **4.** 1,932 R14   **5.** 3,748 R3

6. 6,565 R4   **7.** 6,059 R3   **8.** 807 R16   **9.** 14,209 R0   **10.** 5,258 R9

11. 4,965 R0   **12.** 4,935 R2   **13.** 4,210 R4   **14.** 11,293 R1   **15.** 30,457 R1

16. 9,218 R0   **17.** 5,758 R0   **18.** 6,263 R10   **19.** 8,421 R7   **20.** 3,745 R8

Page 6:   Multi Digit Multiplication

1. 40,101,604   **2.** 343,679,054   **3.** 456,105,800   **4.** 62,209,028

5. 202,820,625   **6.** 118,010,744   **7.** 261,253,928   **8.** 206,224,647

9. 82,966,044   **10.** 76,550,775   **11.** 234,585,578   **12.** 53,763,996

13. 493,458,595   **14.** 837,404,700   **15.** 345,915,850   **16.** 173,939,148

17. 286,407,156   **18.** 94,189,164   **19.** 64,142,118   **20.** 121,276,956

21. 218,939,440   **22.** 135,154,368   **23.** 574,712,992   **24.** 207,797,946

25. 114,291,240   **26.** 275,652,930   **27.** 97,571,250

Page 9:   Multi Digit Decimals Multiplication

1. 9,153.8130   **2.** 9,570.3341   **3.** 46,213.9762   **4.** 89,234.5353

5. 6,159.0526   **6.** 35,097.6850   **7.** 78,261.6789   **8.** 18,570.8232

9. 3,130.4253   **10.** 32,470.7496   **11.** 62,916.9345   **12.** 8,966.9892

13. 86,233.8224   **14.** 5,372.1018   **15.** 17,312.5368   **16.** 32,794.5432

17. 9,645.7218   **18.** 13,908.0690   **19.** 29,101.5400   **20.** 23,950.9602

21. 35,840.3172   **22.** 31,329.7845   **23.** 73,826.2245   **24.** 4,112.9032

25. 33,971.8665   **26.** 22,500.8352   **27.** 4,481.2536

Page 12: Dividing Decimals

1. 4.73   **2.** 9.58   **3.** 1.59   **4.** 2.90   **5.** 13.14   **6.** 4.11   **7.** 5.83

8. 11.14   **9.** 43.39   **10.** 6.70   **11.** 12.11   **12.** 17.69   **13.** 2.72   **14.** 8.19

15. 16.30   **16.** 26.41   **17.** 8.44   **18.** 14.20   **19.** 5.19   **20.** 6.00   **21.** 15.82

22. 6.73   **23.** 6.29   **24.** 27.09   **25.** 60.65   **26.** 13.98   **27.** 15.07

Page 15: Place Value

1. 6 hundredths   **2.** 0 ones   **3.** 2 hundreds

4. 0 thousands   **5.** 6 hundredths   **6.** 7 hundred thousands

7. 3 hundreds   **8.** 4 thousandths   **9.** 5 hundreds

10. 3 hundred millions   **11.** 7 ten thousands   **12.** 2 millions

13. 3 tenths   **14.** 9 tenths   **15.** 1 hundred million

16. 7 hundredths   **17.** 9 thousandths   **18.** 0 hundredths

19. 7 ones   **20.** 7 ones   **21.** 5 billions

22. 2 hundreds   **23.** 4 tens   **24.** 9 tenths

25. 3 hundred thousands   **26.** 3 billions   **27.** 2 hundreds

28. 7 tens   **29.** 6 ten thousands   **30.** 6 ten thousands

Page 19: Place Value and Expanded Notation

1. 453,576,455   **2.** 4,865,680.82   **3.** 559,287.922   **4.** 943,792.429

5. 707,128.796   **6.** 30,448,851.7   **7.** 232,781.559   **8.** 742,461.912

9. 204,266,329   **10.** 67,959,822.3   **11.** 234,295.768   **12.** 690,510,169

13. 8,604,527.68   **14.** 52,765,324.9   **15.** 104,245,061   **16.** 251,436,598

17. 576,894.755   **18.** 31,136,893.6   **19.** 480,732.817

Page 24:   Factors

1. 2, 3, 4, 6, 8, 12, 16, 24, 32, 48

2. None

3. 2, 3

4. 2, 3, 5, 6, 10, 15

5. 3, 9, 11, 33

6. 2, 4, 5, 10, 20, 25, 50

7. 3, 13

8. 2, 17

9. 5, 7

10. None

11. None

12. None

13. None

14. 7

15. 2, 4

16. None

17. None

18. 2, 4, 8, 11, 22, 44

19. 2, 4, 8

20. 2, 3, 5, 6, 9, 10, 15, 18, 30, 45

21. 2, 3, 6, 9, 18, 27

22. 3, 23

23. 2, 37

24. 2, 4, 13, 26

25. None

26. 2, 3, 6, 7, 14, 21

27. None

28. None

Page 28:   Multiples

1. 29, 58, 87, 116, 145

2. 8, 16, 24, 32, 40

3. 79, 158, 237, 316, 395

4. 92, 184, 276, 368, 460

5. 67, 134, 201, 268, 335

6. 44, 88, 132, 176, 220

7. 97, 194, 291, 388, 485

8. 71, 142, 213, 284, 355

9. 6, 12, 18, 24, 30

10. 7, 14, 21, 28, 35

11. 4, 8, 12, 16, 20

12. 18, 36, 54, 72, 90

13. 58, 116, 174, 232, 290

14. 22, 44, 66, 88, 110

15. 47, 94, 141, 188, 235

16. 86, 172, 258, 344, 430

17. 50, 100, 150, 200, 250

18. 55, 110, 165, 220, 275

19. 2, 4, 6, 8, 10

20. 1, 2, 3, 4, 5

21. 17, 34, 51, 68, 85

22. 30, 60, 90, 120, 150

23. 21, 42, 63, 84, 105

24. 94, 188, 282, 376, 470

25. 53, 106, 159, 212, 265

26. 52, 104, 156, 208, 260

27. 25, 50, 75, 100, 125

28. 61, 122, 183, 244, 305

29. 60, 120, 180, 240, 300

30. 87, 174, 261, 348, 435

31. 23, 46, 69, 92, 115

32. 48, 96, 144, 192, 240

33. 56, 112, 168, 224, 280

34. 91, 182, 273, 364, 455

35. 76, 152, 228, 304, 380

Page 33: Convert Fractions and Decimals

1. 0.333 **2.** 0.417 **3.** 0.417 **4.** 0.936 **5.** 10/18

6. 0.105 **7.** 0.826 **8.** 0.275 **9.** 9/20 **10.** 5/18

11. 0.667 **12.** 0.14 **13.** 2/5 **14.** 0.071 **15.** 0.3

16. 6/8 **17.** 5/11 **18.** 20/23 **19.** 0.25 **20.** 7/9

21. 0.5 **22.** 27/70 **23.** 0.714 **24.** 0.545 **25.** 0.053

26. 481/1000 **27.** 0.033 **28.** 0.82 **29.** 19/25 **30.** 0.438

31. 0.528 **32.** 12/24 **33.** 0.765 **34.** 0.938 **35.** 0.667

36. 2/15

Page 36:   Mixed Numbers

1. 96/19   **2.** 119/16   **3.** 8 5/11   **4.** 29/6   **5.** 5 1/2

6. 2 4/5   **7.** 25/8   **8.** 20/17   **9.** 11/4   **10.** 17/2

11. 41/5   **12.** 26/7   **13.** 40/19   **14.** 113/36   **15.** 9 2/3

16. 33/5   **17.** 13/8   **18.** 4 2/7   **19.** 17/2   **20.** 51/14

21. 6 1/5   **22.** 9 29/30   **23.** 37/18   **24.** 2 25/36   **25.** 13/2

26. 27/5   **27.** 19/2   **28.** 3 1/3

Page 38:   Mixed Numbers: Addition and Subtraction

1. 2 1/6   **2.** 4 23/36   **3.** 10 51/70   **4.** 4 2/3   **5.** 9 13/15

6. 17 2/21   **7.** 4 28/45   **8.** 1 1/4   **9.** 14 17/30   **10.** 2 29/36

11. 4 1/5   **12.** 1 11/30   **13.** 10 11/12   **14.** 9 1/6   **15.** 8 53/63

16. 1 1/5   **17.** 1   **18.** 7 1/8   **19.** 12 20/21   **20.** 5 25/28

21. 2 11/72   **22.** 3 2/15   **23.** 4   **24.** 1   **25.** 1 27/35

26. 11 19/20

Page 42:   Mixed Numbers: Multiplication and Division

1. 23 1/14   **2.** 1 25/152   **3.** 8 5/9   **4.** 33 1/36   **5.** 34

6. 13 29/40   **7.** 27/50   **8.** 9 1/16   **9.** 2 11/40   **10.** 68 14/15

11. 5 2/15   **12.** 57 1/2   **13.** 8 1/20   **14.** 52 73/90   **15.** 35 29/56

16. 45/164   **17.** 2 7/10   **18.** 31 8/15   **19.** 2 3/7   **20.** 100/133

21. 18 2/7   **22.** 19 19/20   **23.** 1 3/16   **24.** 9/10   **25.** 1 31/35

26. 49 13/15

Page 46: Multiplication with Whole Numbers

1. 4 4/7	**2.** 1/4	**3.** 2 1/2	**4.** 7 1/2	**5.** 1 15/17	**6.** 2 4/5
7. 2 6/7	**8.** 7/9	**9.** 5 1/19	**10.** 2	**11.** 3 3/4	**12.** 3
13. 1 1/4	**14.** 4	**15.** 3/7	**16.** 1 1/3	**17.** 4/5	**18.** 1 1/2
19. 10/13	**20.** 1 1/2	**21.** 1 4/5	**22.** 2/7	**23.** 5 3/5	**24.** 4 1/16
25. 2 14/17	**26.** 9/11	**27.** 1 3/5	**28.** 2 16/19		

Page 48: Simplify Fractions: Proper and Improper Fractions

1. 7	**2.** 7/15	**3.** 7 1/3	**4.** 5	**5.** 2 10/11	**6.** 8 3/4
7. 3 13/18	**8.** 5 1/3	**9.** 1/7	**10.** 6 1/2	**11.** 3/5	**12.** 2/5
13. 9 12/19	**14.** 5/8	**15.** 7 16/17	**16.** 5	**17.** 5	**18.** 2 1/14
19. 5 1/4	**20.** 10/13	**21.** 1/20	**22.** 1/9	**23.** 3	**24.** 7
25. 4	**26.** 9/20	**27.** 8	**28.** 2	**29.** 6	**30.** 5
31. 5	**32.** 5/17	**33.** 2	**34.** 8	**35.** 1/6	**36.** 3 1/2
37. 9 7/9	**38.** 9 3/19	**39.** 4 3/4	**40.** 6 1/2	**41.** 5	**42.** 11/12

Page 51: Area and Perimeter

1. P=34.2 A=56.28	**2.** P=60.84 A=161.2548
3. P=25.33 A=27.36	**4.** P=47.3 A=106.94
5. P=21.4 A=17.22	**6.** P=22.9 A=24.47
7. P=60.48 A=227.9744	**8.** P=48.16 A=84.5696
9. P=31.2 A=46.84	**10.** P=38.16 A=65.2536
11. P=44.94 A=106.0752	**12.** P=29.60 A=35.535
13. P=39.3 A=57.13	**14.** P=17.1 A=13.69

15. P=44.64 A=124.5440

16. P=64.08 A=201.4227

17. P=63.04 A=248.3200

18. P=28.0 A=37.19

19. P=33.5 A=49.96

20. P=33.9 A=39.22

21. P=64.98 A=152.2071

22. P=45.44 A=88.4

23. P=21.2 A=18.92

24. P=33.80 A=70.5000

25. P=38.88 A=64.9

26. P=21.9 A=21.94

27. P=35.52 A=78.8220

28. P=47.41 A=96.48

Page 58: Area and Circumference

1. C=18.84 cm A=28.26 cm^2

2. C=6.28 cm A=3.14 cm^2

3. C=62.80 cm A=314.00 cm^2

4. C=81.64 cm A=530.66 cm^2

5. C=12.56 cm A=12.56 cm^2

6. C=125.60 cm A=1,256.00 cm^2

7. C=113.04 cm A=1,017.36 cm^2

8. C=31.40 cm A=78.50 cm^2

9. C=37.68 cm A=113.04 cm^2

10. C=119.32 cm A=1,133.54 cm^2

11. C=69.08 cm A=379.94 cm^2

12. C=106.76 cm A=907.46 cm^2

13. C=43.96 cm A=153.86 cm^2

14. C=25.12 cm A=50.24 cm^2

15. C=75.36 cm A=452.16 cm^2

16. C=94.20 cm A=706.50 cm^2

17. C=100.48 cm A=803.84 cm^2

18. C=50.24 cm A=200.96 cm^2

19. C=56.52 cm A=254.34 cm^2

20. C=87.92 cm A=615.44 cm^2

21. C=94.20 cm A=706.50 cm^2

22. C=6.28 cm A=3.14 cm^2

23. C=125.60 cm A=1,256.00 cm^2

24. C=56.52 cm A=254.34 cm^2

25. C=81.64 cm A=530.66 cm^2

26. C=25.12 cm A=50.24 cm^2

27. C=113.04 cm A=1,017.36 cm^2

28. C=113.04 cm A=1,017.36 cm^2

Page 65:   Measuring Angles

1. 100° Obtuse	**2.** 90° Right	**3.** 110° Obtuse	**4.** 50° Acute
5. 140° Obtuse	**6.** 100° Obtuse	**7.** 90° Right	**8.** 60° Acute
9. 70° Acute	**10.** 30° Acute	**11.** 170° Obtuse	**12.** 160° Obtuse
13. 80° Acute	**14.** 120° Obtuse	**15.** 20° Acute	**16.** 160° Obtuse
17. 110° Obtuse	**18.** 70° Acute	**19.** 20° Acute	**20.** 140° Obtuse

Page 70:   Volume and Surface Area

1. V=252 in³ in³ SA=240 in² in²

2. V=96 ft³ ft³ SA=128 ft² ft²

3. V=720 cm³ cm³ SA=484 cm² cm²

4. V=351.86 ft³ ft³ SA=276 ft² ft²

5. V=120 ft³ ft³ SA=148 ft² ft²

6. V=169.65 ft³ ft³ SA=170 ft² ft²

7. V=18 in³ in³ SA=42 in² in²

8. V=6.28 ft³ ft³ SA=19 ft² ft²

9. V=392 cm³ cm³ SA=322 cm² cm²

10. V=141.37 in³ in³ SA=151 in² in²

11. V=75 cm³ cm³ SA=110 cm² cm²

12. V=28.27 cm³ cm³ SA=52 cm² cm²

13. V=48 in³ in³ SA=80 in² in²

14. V=80 in³ in³ SA=112 in² in²

15. V=150 cm³ cm³ SA=170 cm² cm²

16. V=120 cm³ cm³ SA=148 cm² cm²

17. V=282.74 in³ in³ SA=245 in² in²

18. V=216 in³ in³ SA=216 in² in²

19. V=60 in³ in³ SA=94 in² in²

20. V=210 in³ in³ SA=214 in² in²

Page 75:   Metric Weights and Measures

1. 0.046	**2.** 0.025	**3.** 39,000	**4.** 60,000	**5.** 0.082	**6.** 21,000
7. 0.013	**8.** 0.019	**9.** 62,000	**10.** 33,000	**11.** 77,000	**12.** 0.060
13. 97,000	**14.** 0.036	**15.** 80,000	**16.** 53,000	**17.** 0.085	**18.** 0.052
19. 90,000	**20.** 55,000	**21.** 62,000	**22.** 63,000	**23.** 0.029	**24.** 33,000

25. 11,000   **26.** 0.012   **27.** 0.048   **28.** 10,000   **29.** 42,000   **30.** 71,000

Page 77:   Mean and Median

1. Mean = 64, Median = 80

2. Mean = 49.333, Median = 48.5

3. Mean = 40.333, Median = 34

4. Mean = 63.333, Median = 70

5. Mean = 41.333, Median = 43.5

6. Mean = 37, Median = 28.5

7. Mean = 51.167, Median = 38.5

8. Mean = 52.167, Median = 54.5

9. Mean = 69.5, Median = 81.5

10. Mean = 46.5, Median = 45.5

11. Mean = 40.667, Median = 33.5

12. Mean = 71.333, Median = 76.5

13. Mean = 61.167, Median = 56.5

14. Mean = 57.833, Median = 66

15. Mean = 45.5, Median = 43.5

16. Mean = 32.667, Median = 39

17. Mean = 53.167, Median = 51

18. Mean = 61.167, Median = 74

19. Mean = 44.833, Median = 38

20. Mean = 45.667, Median = 38

21. Mean = 41.5, Median = 39

22. Mean = 43, Median = 43.5

23. Mean = 53.833, Median = 59

24. Mean = 68.333, Median = 78.5

9 798330 203086